Writing Essays and Research Reports in the Social Sciences

Katharine Betts
Karen Farquharson
Anne Seitz

THOMSON

Australia · Canada · Mexico · Singapore · Spain · United Kingdom · United States

THOMSON

SOCIAL SCIENCE PRESS

Level 7, 80 Dorcas Street
South Melbourne Victoria 3205

Email: highereducation@thomsonlearning.com.au
Website: www.thomsonlearning.com.au

First published in 1986; second edition in 1994; third edition 2005
10 9 8 7 6 5 4 3 2 1
09 08 07 06 05

National Library of Australia
Cataloguing-in-Publication data

Betts, Katharine.
Writing essays and research reports in the social sciences.

> 3rd ed.
> Includes index.
> ISBN 0 17 012794 X.

> 1. English language - Rhetoric. 2. Report writing. 3.
> Social sciences - Research. I. Farquharson, Karen. II.
> Seitz, Anne. III. Title.

808.042

Project editor: Chris Wyness
Publishing editor: Elizabeth Vella
Publishing manager: Michael Tully
Indexer: Julie King
Text designer: Chris Ryan
Cover designer: Olga Lavecchia
Original cover concept: Patrick Jennings
Typeset in New Aster and Gill Sans by Linotype
Production controller: Jodie Van Teyligen
Printed in Australia by Ligare Book Printers

This title is published under the imprint of Thomson/Social Science Press.
Nelson Australia Pty Limited ACN 058 280 149 (incorporated in Victoria)
trading as Thomson Learning Australia.

The URLs contained in this publication were checked for currency during the production process. Note, however, that the publisher cannot vouch for the ongoing currency of URLs.

Contents

Acknowledgements

A number of friends and colleagues have given useful criticism and encouragement when we were working on either the first, second or third edition of this book. Some have been kind enough to help with all three. In particular we would like to thank Diane Austin, Bettina Cass, Bill Foddy, Megan Farquharson, Rebecca Farquharson, Lois Foster, Frances Lovejoy, Helen Marshall, David Mayer, Tim Marjoribanks, Belinda Probert, Ulla Svensson, and Evan Willis. We would especially like to thank Simon Kneebone for his illustrations, Gavin Betts for his glossary, and Samantha Henderson for her research report.

We, however, accept full responsibility for any shortcomings that may be present.

Chapter 1

Introduction

Many students are confused and uncertain when they start to write their first essay at university. They do not know what is expected of them and they are not sure that they can do it anyway. So if you feel like this you are not alone.

Your assessment at university depends very much on your written work. This book is designed to help you master the skills involved in organising your ideas and presenting them in a convincing way. We will approach this at two levels: the conceptual and the practical. This means that we will talk about planning, thinking, formulating opinions and arguing, but we will also discuss the practical questions of reading, organising your notes, documenting your material, and the question of what to do when you try to write and nothing seems to happen.

We are starting from first principles. We assume that you are a first-year student and not so confident or experienced as to be offended by some rather basic advice. But while the advice may be basic, it will not be superseded. You will continue to build on these fundamental skills as you go on with your studies as, for example, when you are planning a research project and writing it up, or organising your ideas for a minor thesis and accumulating the large body of material that this will require. The processes of scholarship are similar at all levels. If you learn to be systematic in first year, and if you understand why the processes are important, fourth year will not be harder. It will just be more interesting.

Riding the electronic wave: computers and the written word

In this book we take it for granted that you already have basic computer skills and that you know their advantages. With computers you can organise your knowledge and ideas more easily than with pen and paper, speed up your writing, improve your spelling and presentation, and enjoy yourself at the same time. You can work through three, five, or 25 drafts of the same document without writing it (or typing it) three, five or 25 times. You can write an essay and hand it in and still have it; you can write a letter and post it and still keep it. You can organise your references, store your data, do your calculations. You can make your printouts look professional. You can even play with making them look beautiful, and you don't even need to be a good typist.

For the most part, your lecturers will expect you to submit work that has been prepared on a computer, and many will also expect you to do the library research for your essays on a networked computer. Indeed, almost all universities nowadays provide networked computers for their students to use, and most university computer systems are accessible from home if you have your own computer and Internet access. You will find your computer (or the one at your university) indispensable for most of your classes.

What if you aren't confident about using a computer for writing or research? Don't worry—help is available. Most universities provide coaching for new students on both how to use computers for word processing, and how to use them for research. Find out about the computer facilities on your campus. If you need some help, ask at the library, the Faculty Office, the student union. Ask your tutor. Try off-campus. Ask at the Council library, the local 'Neighbourhood House' or learning centre, the Council of Adult Education. Most of the programs students need for their work are now easier to use than ever. (Using a computer for social research is discussed further in Chapter 3.)

The aims of this book

The computer is just a tool to help us get practical tasks done quickly and efficiently. It has little to do with the ability to plan, think, read and understand, to structure an argument and to ground it in objectively available evidence. The following chapters are devoted just as much to these conceptual skills as to the practical ones.

We will discuss these conceptual skills using examples drawn from sociology, because that is the subject we teach and know best, but they are not exclusive to sociology. The principles which the examples illustrate apply throughout the social sciences. Indeed the principles are not even exclusive to the world of higher education. Long after your formal studies are over and much of the content of your courses has faded from your attention, it will be these approaches to arguing and using evidence that will stay with you.

But that is for the future. At the moment you are concerned with the immediate task of approaching your first piece of written work. Rather than talking about the principles of scholarly discourse in an abstract and theoretical way, we will talk first about your assignment and use it as an example of these principles. We are guessing that this first paper will be an essay and that research reports will come later. (If we are wrong, and you are being asked to begin with a research report, you will need to read on ahead to Chapter 6.)

This is a book about writing essays and research reports. It is not an introduction to the subject matter of the social sciences. There are a number of good introductions available. Macionis (2004) is a North American work on sociology while Giddens (2001) is British. Holmes et al. (2003) provides an Australian introduction to sociology, while Macionis and Plummer (2002) combine American and British approaches to sociology. Boreham at al. (2004) provide a clear, comprehensive introduction to Australian politics. All of these are substantial texts. In contrast, Berger (1966) and Willis (2004) are brief, clearly-expressed overviews of the sociological approach. Willis's book, *The Sociological Quest*, is a particularly useful point of departure for students in Australia and New Zealand; it uses many local examples and presents key issues in social theory in a straight-forward fashion. Any of these books will help you gain a feel for the subject matter and some, like Macionis and Plummer (2002) and Holmes et al. (2003), contain review questions or hints on how to study.

Though our book is not a general 'how to study' guide, the skills involved in working on research projects and writing essays do not exist in isolation. We will try to put them into context for you which means talking about reading, taking part in tutorials, using the library, managing your time and interacting with staff.

Tutors and tutorials

Universities are less personal than schools and, as they expand to take in ever more students, this impersonality may be increasing. When numbers are large it can be hard for students to get to know each other, and hard for lecturers and tutors to get know them too. Some people find the larger scale of university life exciting, others find it alienating. Most of those who find it exciting have discovered some way of making it less impersonal. They realise that they have to work a little harder at building relationships with other students, and with lecturers and tutors. If you can build these relationships you will be happier, which is a good thing in itself, and you will be able to work more effectively.

How do you get to know other students? The quick, sure way is to join some clubs. But try talking to them before and after classes and during tutorials; you have your work in common and probably a lot more as well. As far as study is concerned, the 'tutorials' that go on in the cafeteria after the class are often the most useful of all.

How do you get to know the staff and help them to get to know you? Before we answer that question we should explain who the staff are and how we will refer to them here. There are staff who lecture, staff who give tutorials, and staff who do both. People called 'professor', 'associate professor', 'reader', 'senior lecturer' and 'lecturer' will give lectures and most of them will also run some tutorials. There are some staff, often post-graduate students working part-time, who are called 'tutors' and who only give tutorials. But if a professor is conducting your tutorial, he or she is your 'tutor' and will probably mark your essays. Throughout this book we will use the term 'tutor' to describe the person marking your work, irrespective of that person's academic rank.

Most university teachers care about their students but large classes make it difficult for them to show this. This is especially true in large lectures. For their part, it is easy for students to treat the lecturer as a television set, a remote talking head. But the opportunity for personal contact between students and staff arises more often in tutorials than it does in lectures. Make it easier for tutors to know who you are by taking part in tutorial discussions. If you are terrified of speaking out, you can go to see the tutor privately and explain this.

Many students are worried about taking up too much of a tutor's time, just as they are worried about speaking too much, or too little, in tutorials. Let's take the last concern first. Tutorials are like a guided conversation. In a conversation you don't want to monopolise the airwaves and you don't want to be a wallflower; it's the same with tutorials. Here is a simple rule: if you are worried about whether you are speaking too much, you probably are not. In our experience, the few students who go on and on have not learnt to reflect on their behaviour; it simply hasn't occurred to them to wonder if they are taking up more than their fair share of the conversation. But people who don't speak at all are certainly not taking part. If it's difficult for you to join in, try preparing at least one question or comment before the class. When you know what you are going to say it's easier to break the ice. (Reading and preparing for tutorials are discussed further in Chapter 3 under **Taking notes**.)

What about the private chat with the tutor? Observe his or her set times for consultations, unless it's an emergency, and don't stay longer than a quarter of an hour unless this is really necessary. If you have a number of questions to ask, write them down. This might sound a bit formal, but the 'doctor's surgery' syndrome sometimes set in. Though you are sure you have more to say, mild stage fright can drive it from your mind. Many tutors are also willing to answer questions by email and may even prefer to arrange meetings by email. Your tutor will let you know how he or she would like to be contacted. In any case, you don't need to have a private consultation to get to know your tutor; active participation in tutorials helps you to understand the subject and builds personal bridges as well. We hope, too, that the advice that we offer in this book will cut down on the need for individual consultations because, nine times out of ten, the question a student asks is: 'How am I going to write this essay?'

Look on this book as something between a life preserver and a navigation aid. It will keep you afloat while you learn to swim in a sea of words, lectures and tutorials. It will help you to find your way to the pleasant island of the finished final draft. There on the sunny beach you can contemplate your final achievement, the knowledge organised into well-crafted paragraphs, the ideas linked and well-expressed. You can pause for a while and wonder why you were ever afraid of the ocean of knowledge. You did not drown. You had the skills to discover and use its currents, winds and directions, and to find your way about in it as comfortably as anyone else.

Chapter 2

Beginning at the beginning

Answering the question

What is the essay topic asking you to do? You must be sure you understand this before you make a start. If possible, sit down with some friends who are taking the same subject and talk about what you think the question means. Try to get a clear picture of the key concepts before you go to the library.

In the social sciences, topics may relate directly to social and political life itself and ask questions about, for example, power relations within families, or the origins of social movements, or the causes of inequality between nations, or of unemployment, or of immigration. Other kinds of topics ask you to write about the theories that have been developed to explain that social and political reality. What did Touraine write about social movements or Parkin about class and status groups? The wording of the actual question can vary. You may be asked to 'outline', 'discuss', 'explain', 'compare and contrast', 'account for' or 'critically assess'. But in spite of this variation in the way they are expressed, most questions can be understood as variations on four basic themes: description, analysis, explanation and evaluation.

An essay that asks you to 'outline the development of green politics in Australia' is asking you to describe what happened. What were the main events and organisations, who were the key people who took part, what were the most important outcomes? In most instances, however, a descriptive account is only the first step. The question will usually ask you to go further – to analyse and explain.

What does this mean?

'Analysing', in the context of the question about the green politics, means thinking more clearly about those words: 'main', 'key' and 'most important'. Why did you select those events and those people and those outcomes in your descriptive account? What are these more significant aspects of the green movement that you have decided to focus on? Perhaps they include the kinds of people who vote for 'green' candidates, sign petitions and attend demonstrations, or they may include the kinds of people who become devoted activists, spending a large part of their time working in and for environmental organisations. Which environmental organisations will count most in your description? Maybe Greenpeace is in, but what about the 'Friends of the Valley Reserve'? What about the opposition? Many groups and individuals disagree with environmentalists; is it important to describe them and their actions? What about the social and political structures that provide the setting for green politics? – the law, the major political parties, parliament, the mass media, big corporations, unions, the market place. Do school children count?

You can't even begin to describe all of this. You have to be selective. There are practical reasons for selection: you've given yourself just over two weeks to work on this essay, it has a 2000 word limit and, in any case, you have a psychology experiment to write up as well. But the conceptual reasons for being selective are more important. Analysing means choosing the more important elements of the situation and being aware of why you have chosen them. Often your reasons for selecting certain aspects of the problem will relate to the explanation for the phenomenon that you were working on. You found that if you were to explain why the green movement has occurred, you had to look more closely at some aspects of it than others. Analysis and explanation can go hand in hand. Maybe the school children taking part in local activities like the Valley Reserve working bees (picking up garbage and planting native plants) were important. Why? Because, in your view, green activism is largely regionalised and small scale. (Your essay will go on to develop and explore this argument.)

Essays about social theory (rather than aspects of social reality) can also be descriptive. A descriptive essay on, for example, rational choice theory would require you to list and describe the various ideas expressed by rational choice theorists. In contrast, an analytical essay involves you in identifying 'key' or 'major' ideas and specifying the criteria you used when you decided that these particular ideas were more important than others. But just as topics that begin with social life itself usually require analysis and explanation, so those that begin with social theory usually require analysis and evaluation. This means that you have to be critical.

Being critical does not mean thinking of all the negative things you can say about an author or theory. It means that you give your reasons for accepting or rejecting the ideas, that you spell out the criteria you are using in making judgements. Is this theory logical? Is it internally consistent? Is it well grounded in convincing evidence? Does it explain events more comprehensively than other theories? A critical evaluation does not have to be negative. It could be complimentary, or you could decide that the ideas were ill-founded and absurd. You can't tell how it will turn out till you try.

So before you begin work on your essay, decide whether the question is asking you to write about some aspect of social reality or whether it is asking you to write about theories that have been developed by other people to explain that reality. In the first case your essay will very likely take the form of describing what is happening and trying to explain why. Here *you* are being the social theorist. In the second case you'll be describing someone else's social theories and, probably, giving your opinion of these theories. Most essay topics either clearly fall into one of these two categories or combine them. For example, if you were asked to write a book review this would be an example of a 'theory' essay because you would write a critical evaluation. If you were asked to carry out some primary research of your own and write a report on it this would be an example of an essay about an aspect of 'social reality'.

Essay topics are sometimes set in a form which asks you to look at one phenomenon in terms of another: 'The growing use of company cars as a benefit given to senior staff is linked to a decline in official support for public transport. Discuss.' Questions like this are really questions asking you to explain an aspect of social reality. If you accept the claim that official support for public transport has declined, is the practice of rewarding senior staff with company cars a useful way of explaining this decline? Or are other factors more important?

Other 'social reality' questions may ask you to look at the effects of a phenomenon. 'Rising divorce rates and the growing incidence of one-parent families are linked with an increase in juvenile crime.

Discuss.' You could approach this question by focusing on the effects of one-parent families, especially those created by divorce, on children. This would mean that you were writing an essay that was more about the effects of a social phenomenon than its causes. Or you could concentrate on the juvenile crime. What causes it, and what role does divorce and the absence of one parent play in these causes? With this approach you'd be working on an explanatory essay.

Essay topics that ask you to 'compare and contrast' may well be examples of topics that combine a social reality question with a critical appraisal of social theories. For example if you are asked to 'compare and contrast the reserve-army theory of Australian immigration with the growth-of-the-domestic-market theory' you are being asked to concentrate on two pre-existing theories that have been developed to explain immigration. To do a neat job you could begin with a brief account of the facts. What is the pattern of immigration to Australia? Then you would go on to try to explain these facts, but your explanation would be constrained by the requirement that you concentrate on the relative merits of two pre-existing theories. When you conclude that one theory is more useful than the other, or that neither provides a complete explanation and we should look at some other ideas, you are weaving your critical analysis of the existing theories in with your own explanation for the events.

Unpacking the topic

You need to work out the type of essay that you are confronting: a 'social reality' essay, a 'social theory' essay, or a combination. If it's not obvious to you, try translating the question into very simple language. Perhaps you have been set this question:

> High rates of per capita consumption in the First World make
> a considerable contribution to environmental stress. How
> can these consumption rates be explained?

What is the question asking you to do? First, as all essay topics must do, it is asking you to make a few assumptions before you begin. It implies that there is something called 'environmental stress' and that something called 'high rates of per capita consumption' is, at least, a partial cause of this environmental stress. You will need to be sure that you understand the key concepts in the topic: 'per capita consumption' and 'environmental stress'. If you have trouble with this, check lecture notes, textbooks, the set reading and dictionaries of social and political terms. (See Chapter 7 for some titles.)

What if you have unpacked the question and you are starting to feel ill-at-ease because you think that one or both of these assumptions is manifestly unfounded? You could write an interesting essay explaining why you considered the question to be misleading and obfuscating. Some students are nervous about striking out on their own in this way. Remember, universities are places of intellectual freedom and open discussion. If you have logical arguments and empirical evidence to support your opinion, follow that opinion through. Provided you make your grounds for rejecting the initial assumptions quite clear and show that these are based not on emotion but on reason and evidence, the response, 'this is not a useful question', is indeed a valid 'answer to the question'.

You could go to your tutor with a one-page outline of your argument just to check that you've got enough intellectual ammunition for a serious essay taking this approach. While you prepare this outline, ask yourself if you are writing a 'social reality' essay, maybe one arguing that environmental problems have been overstated, or a 'social reality/ social theory' combined essay. This might explore the problem of why many writers are so concerned about a problem that, in your reasoned opinion, is a minor one.

If you are going to accept the assumptions in the essay question you do have an easier task because further unpacking provides clues about the way to begin. Look at the words. The question claims that there is an environmental problem and that rates of per capita consumption in the First World (rich, Western) nations, have a lot to do with this problem. The second sentence contains the question. It asks you to explain why people in these rich nations consume so much. So it's a 'social reality' question. You are being asked to explain an aspect of social life. The first sentence just sets the scene. This means that you wouldn't write a great deal about 'environmental stress' and the level of per capita consumption in the West and its role, relative to other factors like population growth and inappropriate technology, in causing this stress. You would just write enough on this first sentence to show that you understood the concepts and the assumptions behind the question, and that you had good reasons for accepting the assumptions as a starting point.

The greater part of your essay must focus on the question itself: why is per capita consumption so high? Why do we use so many goods, like packaged food, refrigerators, cars and houses, and so many services, like public transport, education, health care and garbage collection? This will form the main body of your response.

Essays that did not answer the question could take a variety of forms. They might concentrate on documenting environmental problems, or on describing patterns of consumption in minute detail, or on arguing about the rights of other species to share the planet with us, or on Third World population growth, or on a host of other topics. There are many ways of not answering the question. However, it is not true to say that there is only one way of answering it. We have already suggested two: first, saying this is a misconceived question and, for the following reasons, it would be absurd to try to answer it, and second, the more straightforward approach. But as Chapter 4 explains, even a so-called 'straightforward' approach can lead to many different answers.

Talk about your essay as much as you can, both with friends who are taking the same course and with other people as well. Your written work will be a careful argument in which you try to convince your reader that you understand the question and have a serviceable answer to it. You will be more confident about writing it down if you have already talked it out.

Deadlines, expecting the unexpected, and word limits

At school, teachers reminded you about your homework and parents probably tried to keep you up to the mark as well. You worked hard, but other people helped you organise your time.

At university you have to do this for yourself. Write the essay topic on a piece of paper, together with any re-interpretations of it that you find helpful, and pin the paper up somewhere where you will see it often. This will help you to think about the question at odd moments. Add the due date to this notice. You should have at least two dates: the actual due date and an earlier date, the date by which you intend to have the essay finished. Try to make this earlier date as early as possible, at least a week prior to the official date. There are two reasons for this. If you can set your essay aside for a few days before handing it in you will be able to see it with new eyes and make improvements to it. And if you have a few days up your sleeve unforeseen problems like a printer breaking down will not be a problem.

Beside the notice of a particular essay topic, keep a list of all assignments due for the semester. Give each one two dates, the official date and your private one. This calendar will help you keep track of the time you should spend on each project.

Try to keep to the prescribed word limit. You are not expected to count the words paragraph by paragraph but you will find that you soon get a working idea of how many words you write to the page. Try to be more or less on target. Too few words will suggest that you have not read widely enough, too many indicates that you were not able to organise the material efficiently. (Most word-processing programs will automatically count the words for you. This can be rewarding. If the work is going slowly you can stop every quarter of an hour and check the progress you've made. Checking every five minutes is probably counter-productive.)

If you have written too much, you must summarise and edit. Perhaps some material is not relevant, and some can be expressed more concisely? In contrast, if you find you do not have enough material, you will need to go back to the library to strengthen your understanding of the topic and to deepen your argument. Chapters 3, 4 and 7 should help you here.

Why do staff insist on word limits; why shouldn't students write twice as much if they have more to say? One reason, especially important with big classes in first year, is time. Staff are hard pressed and essays that are twice as long may take twice the time to mark. But the more important reason is fairness. If the word limit is 1500 words and someone writes 3000 they may well be able to do a better job than people who stick to the guidelines. If the guidelines were never enforced a vicious circle could be established with some people handing in 10 000 words or more.

Being concise is a talent, useful not just in academic life but outside as well. Politicians and chief executives want short briefing papers, newspaper editors want concise articles, speech writers need to express complex ideas succinctly. Precise, clear writing is a skill that comes with practice. Authors have to learn how to write a useful 1500 word essay just as they have to learn how to write a 60 000 word thesis. So, too short is not good, but neither is too long. And guidelines usually are enforced. (A couple of hundred words either way will usually be forgiven; ask your tutor if you're not sure. The words taken up by the list of references are not included in the total.)

You do need to observe the due date. It is important. Late essays inconvenience tutors and they disadvantage other students. The same principle of fairness applies here too. If some students stay up working till 3 a.m. in order to meet deadlines while others take an extra week and finish at their leisure, the situation is clearly not fair. Because of this most tutors are reluctant to grant extensions except in cases of serious illness or personal crisis. If you need to ask for an extension for such a reason, go to your tutor before the due date and be prepared to document your case with a medical certificate or a letter from the student counsellor. Most departments deduct marks from late essays that have not been granted extensions.

Reading, thinking, and developing your ideas all take time, and time is a scarce resource. You need to organise what you have of it and ration it carefully. The calendar with its dual dates is a good tool. Aim to get a final draft of each assignment done by the earlier date. If all goes well you will have six days to put it aside. This means that you will be able to revise it on the seventh day, coming back to it with a clear mind and a fresh eye. If the worst happens and you fall behind with your schedule, the extra week is there as a reserve.

Activities

1. Look at all of the assignments you have for the semester. For the ones that are essays, write down whether the essay is asking you to explain something or whether it is asking you to critically evaluate something.
2. At the beginning of the semester, list all of your assignments and when they are due. For each assignment:
   - Give yourself a private due date that is earlier than the actual due date, to allow for revisions and for unforeseen circumstances.
   - Put the private due dates on a calendar and use them to organise your time so that your assignments will be written by the private due dates.

Chapter 3
Reading and taking notes

Objectives
➤ To learn strategies for locating references for essays
➤ To learn strategies for taking notes on your readings
➤ To understand how to construct a bibliographic filing system

Outline
➤ Wide or deep? Reading wisely
➤ Locating references: reading lists and catalogues
➤ Online databases
➤ Using the Internet for social research
➤ Government publications
➤ Taking notes
➤ Controlling extensive notes
➤ Recording full bibliographic details
➤ Bibliography files
➤ Speed reading and serious reading
➤ The critical appraisal

Wide or deep? Reading wisely

Students often ask, 'How much should I read?' They are likely to get two kinds of answer: 'as much as is necessary', or 'as much as you want to read'. Both seem unhelpful, but they do reflect two different approaches. When you are working to a deadline and an essay of a certain type and length must be produced you have to be focused. Some time should be spent skimming and browsing, and then you should get down to business. Most of this chapter is about this kind of reading: how to do it efficiently and effectively, and how to do as much as is necessary for the task in hand. One way of deciding if you have read enough for a particular essay is to ask yourself if you now understand the question and the concepts it draws on. If you can talk about the ideas involved with reasonable confidence you have probably read enough to write your first draft.

But often students have a different goal in mind when they ask about reading. The subject they are studying intrigues them. They want to master it, not just to get good marks, but so that they can feel they have fully entered into a new area of knowledge. They want to be able to understand how their world works more completely than before. When you ask the question with this goal in mind you get the answer: 'as much as you want to read', but you must want with some passion.

Choose an aspect of your studies that puzzles or fascinates you and read everything about it that you can find. Bury yourself in it. Live it. Perhaps it's Aboriginal studies, perhaps it's feminism, perhaps it's disability, stigma and the management of spoiled identity. Whatever the topic, whether you intend this or not, reading about it in this way will lead you to a deeper understanding of the social sciences. You cannot learn a foreign language just by studying the grammar and memorising lists of words; you must find a book in that language that you really want to read or a native speaker who you really want to talk to. As you work hard to reach that specific goal, the language comes to you. So it is with other fields of study.

When are you going to do this reading that is wide, deep and fervent? In the weekends, on the train, in the evenings, and in the long vacations. For the meantime there are more practical goals. And first you have to learn how to find the books.

Locating references: reading lists and catalogues

Get to know your library. It may seem dauntingly large at first but you must make friends with it quickly. The librarians understand the difficulty. Often they conduct tours during 'orientation week' at the start of the year and have a number of 'reader education' services. Ask about them, find out what is available, and do your own exploring. You can only learn to swim when you feel confident in the water.

The reading list or study guide for your subject is usually the best place to begin your search for readings. Subject coordinators are human and their theories of teaching differ. Consequently reading lists vary. Some are brief, with few references. The principle here is that you are meant to read everything. Others are long, with many references, notes on the sources, study questions, background information, cartoons, computer graphics (and maybe even library catalogue numbers). The principle here is that you are meant to treat the reading list as a mini-version of the library's catalogue and to select material from it. Ask if you're not sure.

Compared with any kind of study guide, library catalogues are enormous lists. They include all of the books and journals in the library and maybe those in some associated libraries as well. Library catalogues used to consist of cards, with at least two entries for most items, one arranged by author and the other by subject, with perhaps a third for titles of books. Now almost all libraries have computerised online catalogues. These virtual catalogues are available within the library from its own computers, and you can often also access them off-campus through the Internet. Here each book or journal will probably only have one 'entry' but you access it in a number of ways: by author, subject, title, key words, the number of your subject code, your lecturer's name and so on. When you first learn to search the online catalogue you may need the librarian's help, but once you understand the basics, you'll find heaps of information at your fingertips.

You will most often use the library to find books and journal articles. If you're looking for a book, you will find that the catalogue gives you a call number. This is the book's 'address' on the library shelves and it should, in principle, allow you to walk right up to your quarry, pick it up, and either read it on the spot or borrow it for later. What if it's not there? Most university libraries have a 'counter reserve' system where works that are in heavy demand can be lent out for a couple of hours. In this way everyone gets a turn, however brief. Your reading list may tell you if a particular book is on counter reserve and a computerised catalogue will probably tell you this too. Even if you don't know, it's always worth asking. Write down the call number and go and ask the librarian in charge of counter reserve. A computer catalogue can also tell you if a book has been borrowed and when it is due back. You may be able to ask to have it held for you when it's returned.

There are two sorts of books in the library: monographs and edited collections. A monograph is the type of book you are probably most used to using: a book written by one or more authors who are responsible for the entire text. Edited collections look like books – they have two covers, a table of contents, and chapters – but they are different from monographs. In edited books, the editor (or editors) will have asked other authors to contribute chapters, so each chapter has its own author or authors and, often, its own topic. Students should think of each chapter of an edited book as a separate publication. But edited books are listed in the library catalogues under the editor or editors' names, not the chapter authors' names. Some online databases (these are discussed below), such as Sociological Abstracts, will allow you to search for chapters in edited books.

Unfortunately, locating references is not just a question of learning to use the library catalogue and finding your way around the book stacks. Other people are trying to use the same books; the printed word has become a scare resource. Each library will have worked out its own system for rationing scarcity. You have to learn this system as well as how to use the catalogue. (You will also find out the rules about booking personal computers, if the library has them, or discussion rooms for group study, and rules about places where talking is permitted and where it is not. Silence is a scarce resource too. You need it just as much as you need time and books.)

What happens if the book you want is not on the shelves and is not on counter reserve and you want it now? It could be half way back to its rightful place, resting in the sorting shelves. If you are allowed access to them, look for it there. And ask a librarian. This is always the first step if, after an honest attempt on your own, you are still stuck.

But perhaps the book is out on loan, or even lost. Try not to panic. All cataloguing systems arrange books by subject, so go to the place on the shelves where your volume should have been and look for other material on the topic. Ask your tutor if this other material is acceptable as a substitute or, if not, whether he or she can suggest some other suitable readings. (If a key book on the reading list is missing, or out on loan when one might have expected it to be on counter reserve, your tutor will want to know.)

The library catalogue will also direct you to reference materials such as dictionaries, encyclopaedias, indexes and abstracts. Many libraries provide online access to subject dictionaries (such as sociology or political science dictionaries) and encyclopaedias. These can be useful if your essay is on an unfamiliar topic, for example, postmodernism, and you really don't understand what it is about. You can look up the topic in a subject dictionary and get a reasonable definition of it.

Online databases

Imagine for a moment that you don't have a reading list. You are on your own trying to find material on a particular topic. How do you start? It may seem obvious to begin with the library catalogue and to search by subject terms, and this is in fact a good way to begin. Try different ways of labelling your topic. Does 'green politics' bring results? What happens if you look up 'ecologists' or 'social movements' or 'environmentalism' or 'conservation'? You will almost certainly get some leads if you make a number of starts. But the library catalogue can only take you a certain distance. This is because it only lists books as a whole, or journals as a whole. It doesn't tell you about their constituent parts.

The problem is obvious with journals. You want to know more about migration from Mexico into the United States. The catalogue tells you that your library keeps a journal called *The International Migration Review*, in many, many volumes going back to 1964. If you went to the shelves and read the title pages of all the issues of the journal to see if you could find some relevant articles, it could take a week.

The library catalogue cannot lead you to journal articles or chapters in edited collections. One way to look for these sources is to check the list of references in material that you do have. What articles and chapters have these authors used? Do any look promising? It makes sense to start with the most recently published material in them because a recent work on your topic will probably refer to older sources and give you some idea of their relevance. But you are not restricted to hunting through lists of other people's sources. The library has a way to help you. You can find journal articles online, by searching the online databases.

University libraries (and most public libraries) subscribe to online databases that you can search to find relevant information for your essays. These databases have made the task of locating information much easier for students and other researchers because they allow you to search the contents of many different publications at the same time. The way this works is that your library will subscribe to one or more databases that include information about groups of publications. You can access these databases through links on your library's computer homepage. These databases usually include articles from magazines, newspapers, and academic journals, and you can search them by entering key words, subjects or authors' names.

All of these databases are searchable. Popular databases for social science include EBSCOHost, InfoTrac, ProQuest and Ingenta. For Australian students, the Australian Public Affairs–Full Text is very useful as it links to the full text of many Australian publications that are often not available elsewhere. You will find it in the Informit database, along with many other Australian sources.

Before you start searching online databases you need to identify the key concepts in your topic. For example, if your assignment is to write an essay about 'green politics,' you will need to think about what that means. Does it mean the Greens political party? Or the social movements focused on the environment? Or something else? Once you've worked out what your topic is, you need to think of different ways it might be expressed and list them. If it is about social movements focused on the environment, you might list: green politics, environmental movement, conservation, environmental politics, and perhaps other related terms. These are the terms you are going to enter into the search field of the online databases.

Once you've listed your search terms, open a database and search it using these terms. The results will be a list of titles of articles. If a title sounds promising, click on it and, most often, some information describing what it is about will appear. Perhaps the search didn't bring up the types of articles that you hoped for? If that's the case, try different search terms from your list. For the topic of youth poverty, you could try 'youth poverty' or 'low income' or 'youth unemployment'; each would yield different results. If you know of an author who has written on your topic, you can search for that author's name, to see if there is anything else they have written. The number of search terms you can use for a particular topic are really only limited by your imagination.

Different databases have different rules about how to format searches. The way you enter your search terms (also known as the syntax you use) does affect the types of articles you will find. Each of the databases has a link to a help page which provides information about how to word searches for that particular database.

Not all online databases have the full text of the articles they list – some of them only contain the abstracts. An abstract is a brief summary of what an article is about. They are useful because they give you a good idea of whether the article will be relevant to your topic or not (more on this later in this chapter). After reading the abstract you should be able to gauge whether the full text of the article is worth pursuing.

So, you've done your search and you've located some promising looking abstracts. What next? Next you need to get the full text version of each article. (For most academic social science articles, the full text version will be between 10 and 50 pages long.) Does the database where you found the abstract provide a link to the full text of the actual article? If it does – great, go ahead and open the article! You can either print a copy, or look at it on the screen. We recommend printing it – that way you can easily refer back to it if you need to.

What if the database doesn't give you access to the article? If that happens you need to check to see whether your library subscribes to the journal where the article is. Some databases provide a 'search the library for this publication' link. If this particular one doesn't, your best bet is to check the library catalogue to see whether your library has access, and if it does, what sort of access is available. Your library may actually have a print version of the journal, or they may provide access to the journal in a different database.

If your library doesn't subscribe to the publication, it can usually be requested from the interlibrary loan section of the library. However, this may take some time, and if your essay is due soon, it is probably best to look for more accessible references.

The articles you locate will vary in quality and credibility. Some will be from newspapers, others from popular magazines, and some will be from peer-reviewed journals. A peer-reviewed journal is a publication where articles are reviewed by experts in the field before they are published, a form of quality control. This means that the information in peer-reviewed journals is usually more credible than information from magazines and other publications. Most of the articles you use for your essays should come from peer-reviewed sources, and many online databases have the option of limiting searches to peer-reviewed titles only.

Online databases are excellent sources for essay materials. They should be one of your first ports of call when researching an essay. If your university does not subscribe to online databases, you should be able to find similar information in books called indexes and abstracts. If you're having trouble finding references, ask your librarian. Most librarians are very happy to help students.

Using the Internet for social research

Many online databases can be accessed via the Internet. You can also search the Internet itself for information on your topic. There is a great deal of information there and it is a potentially useful place to do research for your social science essays. However, if you choose to go down this path, you need to do so carefully: at the end of the trail there is indeed some useful information, but there is a lot of rubbish. The results of academic studies are usually published in peer-reviewed publications and are not available on the Internet. These must almost always be accessed through libraries and/or online databases. The types of useful information that you might be able to get from the Internet include: government reports, company reports, laws, legal judgements, current events news, and conference proceedings. You may also be able to find discussion groups where you can discuss your topic and ask for help.

Before you decide to search the Internet for your topic, think about whether the types of information available there will be useful. Maybe your tutor has said that all of your references should be from academic sources. If so, doing an Internet search for your topic will probably not be useful. However, the Internet can provide background information and some of the information there might be helpful for your essay.

If you decide to use the Internet for your research, you need a search strategy. Essentially, you will be doing keyword searches, so decide what your keywords are. This is similar to entering search terms into online databases. You also need to decide which bits of the Internet you are going to search. Three options to explore are: subject directories, search engines and metasearch engines.

Subject directories (web pages organised by subject, such as those provided by yahoo.com or looksmart.com) organise web pages into subject areas, and can be useful if you have a specific subject in mind. Search engines, like google.com, or sensis.com.au, allow you to enter a search term and retrieve the addresses of web pages that contain the search term. If you have a fairly narrow topic, or want to find a large number of web pages on your topic, a search engine is useful. Finally, metasearch engines, like search.com or metacrawler.com, search multiple search engines at the same time. They then bring the results of these multiple, simultaneous searches together into a list. Metasearch engines can be useful if you have a narrow topic, or if you want a general idea of what is available.

Internet researchers use all of these options. You may find that you are most comfortable using a subject directory first, and then a metasearch engine. Or you may find that Google is all you need. Try all three and see which you find most useful.

The most important consideration when using the Internet for research is the quality of the material available on the web. Anyone who has access to a server can put up anything they like. This means that the information on the web needs to be carefully evaluated. Questions you should ask when using information from a website include: What is the purpose of the website, why does it exist? Has it been created to advocate for a particular position? Who are its authors and can they be contacted? Is it associated with a reputable organisation? Does it provide information that backs up the claims it is making? And, does it list a date when it was last updated? If yes, how long ago was that?

Company websites and government websites can be good sources for official documents such as annual reports and other reports, but they should also be viewed with a critical eye. Private companies may use their sites for marketing purposes, so the items they include are likely to be favourable to their interests. You should also be aware that search engines are not neutral; companies can pay fees to search engines for their websites to be displayed prominently.

There are numerous discussion groups on the Internet that might be able to provide you with information about your topic. You might be able to find useful pointers from them. However, getting involved with Internet discussions is often quite time-consuming, and you will need to consider whether it's worth your while. Internet discussion groups can be found through any of the three options described above.

While the Internet can be a useful tool for social science research, we need to be careful about the kinds of information we take from it. For most research purposes, online databases and library catalogues are better sources of information.

Government publications

The Australian Government, like the governments of all other modern states, produces many publications: reports of Royal Commissions and other special committees of inquiry; parliamentary papers (including the annual reports of government departments); and bulletins produced by the Australian Bureau of Statistics (ABS). Technically, some, like the reports of commissions of inquiry, are monographs. Others are *journals* (or *serials*) because they come out regularly in the same kind of format but with up-dated information. (Just as *monograph* can mean 'book by a single author or authors,' so *serial* can mean *journal*.) A few government publications may even be edited collections. A volume of consultants' reports published with a major report would fall under this heading.

Government publications are all potentially useful to social science students but, partly because they seldom have a named author, they can be hard to track down. Libraries usually shelve them in a separate area and some librarians specialise in managing them. Many of these publications come from a variety of government departments but the ABS is responsible for most of them and it puts out its own catalogue every year in one volume. You can gain a good idea of the range by browsing through any recent Australian *Year Book*, but the ABS catalogue is the comprehensive list. ABS material is also available from the ABS website (<http://www.abs.gov.au>), and the ABS databases can be searched in a similar fashion to other online databases. In fact, libraries are tending to give up their printed holdings of ABS publications and to rely more and more on the online material. Some ABS material on the website is free, but much of it is only available for a fee. However, most Australian universities subscribe to the ABS and, for students of these universities, this means that most of its publications can be downloaded free of charge. It's a fantastic source of information about Australian society. Check with your library to see whether it subscribes.

Other countries collect and publish government statistics. Your library may have year books based on these or it may keep publications put out by the OECD (the Organisation for Economic Cooperation and Development). OECD publications cover statistics for its member nations, all of which are developed countries. United Nations publications have a broader coverage. If you are working on a topic with an international focus, try these, and look for material published by the World Bank and International Monetary Fund as well. Many of these organisations provide free access to their documents via their websites.

The Australian parliamentary papers are a further source of information produced by government. All documents 'tabled' in parliament in Canberra are published and if your library keeps *Hansard*, the record of parliamentary debates, it should keep these as well. They are available to readers in the series of documents called the *Parliamentary Papers* but finding a particular report within this series can be daunting. Remember, there is no shame in asking a librarian for help.

Let's assume that you have collected a number of sources relevant to your essay and are about to begin the attack. What do you do?

Taking notes

The first task is to work at acquiring the art of note-taking. Why take notes? We take notes so that we can accurately record facts, quotes, and ideas that we have read about. We also take notes in order to remember the theme of a work, and our response to it, without necessarily having to go to the trouble of reading the work all over again.

Students who take effective notes on reading for tutorials can run a quick eye over these before the tutorial. They will not be left saying, 'Well, yes, I have read the article [or chapter]. But I did it at the weekend and I can't remember the argument now.' And students with effective notes on the tutorial readings will probably be able to use these notes, if not in the next essay, then in a later one. Taking notes also helps you to understand a piece of writing, to see the structure of an author's ideas, and to evaluate the kinds of evidence used to test these ideas.

How should you go about this note taking? A lot depends on your purpose. Are you skimming a source looking for the date for when women got the vote in South Australia, or are you trying to understand a complex theory on the evolution of family life? The quantity of notes that you need varies with the type of source and the work you want it to do for you. Perhaps you only want to document a particular fact. How many Indochinese refugees did Australia accept in the late 1970s and early 1980s? Look it up (perhaps in Nancy Viviani's book, *The Long Journey*, 1984: 50) and make a note of it. There's no need to read the whole book; just leaf through the chapter headings and use the index. This might take only five minutes. But if you want information about the history of Vietnam, the history of the early outflow of people after the fall of Saigon, Australia's response to the crisis, and what happened to the refugees here in their first few years, you will need to read the whole book and, if it is not your own copy, to take extensive notes.

Whatever your objective, summarising whole books and articles is time-consuming and not often useful. We wish students were rich enough to buy every book they needed, because this allows the best way of making full use of the texts you read. You can write pencilled summaries at the head of chapters, even running summaries at the head of pages if this seems necessary, construct your own 'index' on the front page (where you note themes that are important for your topic and the places where they are discussed), and you can also write your own comments on the job the author has done. (See Chapter 2 on 'evaluation'.) In this way you can make a book really your own and gain a firm grip on the author's argument and your own opinion of its strength. But we know you won't be able to buy as many books as you'd like and that you will have to learn how to take notes from those that are common property in libraries. (Writing in library books is vandalism. But it does happen, and you will often be inconvenienced by the selfishness of the few who abuse common intellectual property in this way.)

Keep your notes to a minimum. Read the chapter or article to the end before you write anything down. It usually helps to 'speed read' it first (see below) and then to reread it seriously. When you have the overall picture you will have a better idea of what is important as far as your needs are concerned. Then you can start take notes. Record the number of the page, or pages, that your notes come from and make it clear to yourself which are your own words and your own ideas and which are those of the author. Always put direct quotes in quotation marks.

You must distinguish between paraphrases of the author's ideas and your own comments on these ideas or indeed your own notes about other thoughts that occur to you as you read. For example, you might wish to explain a concept to yourself in your own words, or something the author says may start you off on a series of reflections of your own. Put your own explanations and remarks in square brackets or use pencil, or a pen with different coloured ink. If you are putting your notes straight into the computer (and why not? – there's no point in writing something out twice) use square brackets or italics for your own ideas. Whatever method you choose, ensure that there will be no chance of confusion between your own ideas, your paraphrases of what the author has said, and direct quotes from the author. When you go back to your notes in a few days time, you may not remember, so make it clear from the very beginning. (Confusion between a student's work and the author's work can lead to accidental plagiarism. See Chapter 5.)

Many students find the photocopier provides a useful compromise between owning a book which they can write in, and making comprehensive notes drawn from the library copy. Making a photocopy can be a practical idea for a chapter (or an article) but not for a whole book. It does have the advantage that you can use a highlighter pen, something that most proud book-buyers are reluctant to do with a real book, however secure their ownership, but one should photocopy in moderation. The earth needs trees, and it is depressing to be submerged in a mass of unread black and grey photocopies. (You should also check the copyright law: this is usually displayed beside the machine.)

Controlling extensive notes

Very occasionally, if the source is really important to you and the book is not your own, your notes may be so lengthy that it would be a good idea to make a summary index of them. Then, later on, you will be able to retrieve the outline of the argument as quickly as possible. Add a top page to your collection of notes, summarising the main points and telling yourself where to find these points in the pages that follow. See the following table to see how such a summary might look.

In this example, the summary is followed by eight pages of notes. Page one of these notes might look like the following table (the actual pages in the article where the ideas came from are carefully recorded in the left-hand margin).

Summary of notes	
Jared Diamond (1997), *Guns, Germs, and Steel: The Fates of Human Societies*, Norton, New York.	See my page number:
Asks: why do some cultural groups come to dominate others? While there's lots of material in between, his answer ultimately depends on their different ability to produce food and thus support larger (or smaller) populations.	1 5
Some groups are lucky in their natural environment and its animals and plants (some can be domesticated and farmed, but most cannot). This means the lucky ones can intensify their food production and increase their numbers.	1–3
Larger populations lead to intermediate factors (such as technology, including guns and steel, but also writing, transport, centralised political organisation, a specialist military plus an evolved resistance to disease).	4
All of these allow them to dominate unlucky groups.	4–5
[I find his answer persuasive. He has lots of evidence and puts his case logically. He considers alternative explanations and he writes clearly.] [I'm intrigued by his ideas about the role of population growth in the development of organised states. Worth coming back to later?]	
He ends by claiming that history is a science, when it's done his way. [I'm not sure about this. Does environmental good luck always lead to domination?]	5

You would only rarely give a source such extensive treatment (perhaps because it was very important to you, or both important and hard to understand). Aim to keep your notes as brief as possible. But be sure to always record full bibliographic details about the source. We have already mentioned page numbers. What else is involved when people ask for 'full bibliographic details'? The answer varies according to whether your source is a book, a chapter in an edited collection of readings, a journal article, or an online source.

Page 1

Page refs	
14	**The question** He starts with the question Yali put to him: 'Why is it that you white people developed so much cargo and brought it to New Guinea, but we black people had little cargo of our own?' [Yali is Papua New Guinea politician. By 'cargo' he means technology, weapons, tinned food, clothing and other supplies that arrive on cargo planes.]
(354)	Diamond later rephrases Yali's question as, '[W]hy did Europeans reach and conquer the lands of Native Americans, instead of vice versa?'
18–22 25	**The answer** He refutes any racial answer based on superior European intelligence. He says Papuans are very smart. He wants to show that the question has an environmental answer.
40 44	Begins with an outline of human evolution and the 'great leap forward' in brain power that all humans experienced 50 000 years ago, which coincided with the human colonization of New Guinea and Australia.
44–5	The occupation of the Americas came later – maybe 35 000 or 13 000 years ago. [Why doesn't he know the date more precisely?]
53–4	Describes the massacre of the peaceful Moriori on the Chatham Islands by the warlike Maori. Says their difference in temperament can't be genetic because both groups were recently descended from the same stock. Uses the tragedy to introduce his environmental argument. The Moriori were a small isolated group of hunter gatherers with simple technology; the Maori were farmers, constantly fighting other Maori, and had developed much better weapons and leadership. [But why didn't the Moriori take up farming? He doesn't say.]
68 74	Moves to a larger scale in analysing the defeat of Atahuallpa, Inca of Peru, and his 80 000 men, by Pizzaro and his 168 Spaniards.
74	Why didn't Atahuallpa go to Spain and capture King Charles 1st? [He puts this question here, answers it on pp.78–80—see below.]
75–77	Goes on to say why Pizzaro won. He had horses, steel weapons, steel armour and guns (the guns weren't much use – but the horses, armour and swords were).
77	Atahuallpa's empire was also weakened by civil war provoked by smallpox. The Spaniards had brought smallpox to America but it got to Peru before they did. [The Spaniards were partly immune to it, through long exposure. The Incas and other native Americans weren't.]

Recording full bibliographic details

You are using four main types of written material: books, chapters in edited collections, journal articles, and online sources. Books, or monographs, are written by one author or a set of two of more authors working as a team to write the whole text, as is the case with the book you are reading now. Almost all the monographs you meet will be clearly recognisable to you as books but not all books are monographs. Remember the edited collections.

If you have been reading a *book* that is a monograph you will need to take a note of:

- the author's name
- the date of the edition you are using
- the title, in italics or underlined
- the publisher
- the place of publication (the town or city, not the country).

If the book has been reprinted many times, and the first edition came out a long time ago, it's a good idea to take a note of the date of the first edition too. This will ensure that you do not make the mistake of assuming that, because your edition of Marx (or Weber, or Durkheim) came out last year, the author is still alive and taking an active part in current debates.

Not all books are monographs; some are edited collections. Edited collections are books where each chapter has its own author or authors. An editor will have gathered up a number of papers from a variety of authors and published them as a book. Each chapter would look like a separate chapter of a standard book, but the authors will be different. If the source is a *chapter in an edited collection*, you will need:

- the chapter author's name
- the date of the edition (of the edited collection) you are using
- the title of the chapter in quotation marks
- the name of the editor or editors
- the title of the book, underlined or in italics
- the publisher
- the place of publication (the town or city, not the country).

This means that, after you have made it clear that your author appeared in such a collection, the rest of the information you need is the same as for a monograph.

If the source is a *journal article* you will need:

- the author's name
- the date of the journal
- the title of the article in quotation marks
- the title of the journal, underlined or in italics

- the volume of the journal
- the number, or issue, of the volume
- the number of the pages where the article begins and ends.

Online sources can be more difficult to keep track of than other types of sources. For many web pages it will not be clear who the author is, who the publisher is, or when the document was published. For online sources you should record:

- the author's name if this is available
- the title of the document in quotation marks
- the date when the page was last modified, if this is available
- the publisher or sponsor of the page, if available
- the URL
- the date you accessed the document

Some online documents, usually downloaded in PDF format, are essentially photocopies of journal articles. For those documents you need to record the same information that you would record for any other journal article. See chapter 5 for more details on how to reference online sources.

For full bibliographic details in every case where there is a named author you need the author's name and initial, but it's also a good idea to write down the first name of the author in full, if it is given, as you might need to know the author's gender. For example, you might want to write: 'Richards claims ...; she also argues that ...'. (Of course first names are not always given, only initials, or the first name may be unfamiliar to you. If this is the case you will have to avoid sentences like this.) Have a look at the section called 'The list of references' in Chapter 5 for some further examples of referencing different types of material.

Bibliography files

It helps you to keep track of the work you have done if you transfer information about your reading into a filing system. You'll want the full bibliographic details, together with some indication of the subject matter. Include information about where you have put your written notes, or your annotated photocopy, so that you can find them again. You can maintain this filing system with cards or you can do it with a computer program. If you are using cards it's best to have two sets: a set of 'author' cards where works are filed by author and a set of 'subject' cards where you list the authors you have read on a particular subject, with their dates. For a modest investment you can buy two card boxes and two packets of index cards and start this system with the very first source you take notes from. We will tell you how to do this in some detail below.

There are also computer programs that serve as bibliographic filing systems. You will need to purchase a program, such as EndNote™ or ProCite™, if you are to use this kind of filing system. (Check whether your university has bought a site licence for one of these programs. It's just possible that, as an enrolled student, you may be able to get a free, or subsidised, copy for your home computer.) Bibliographic programs make a student's life easier because they provide a concise way of keeping track of all the sources you've read. The principles for using bibliographic software are the same as with the card system, but you only need one entry (or record) for each source, instead of two. And you can store quite a lot of the information about the source in the bibliographic record itself. So if you're taking fairly brief notes, you can just put them into the record, along with the other bibliographic details, and store them there. You can even add direct quotes to the individual records which, at a later date, could be lifted out and put into an essay without being retyped. (But be careful; direct quotes should be used sparingly. See Chapter 5.) In the case of resources such as newspaper articles, you may be able to download an electronic copy and paste the whole text into the 'notes' field of the record.

Most bibliographic software runs in tandem with a variety of word-processing packages. When you are ready to use your stored references in your essay, they can be inserted into the essay with a simple click of the mouse, and your reference list will be automatically generated by the bibliographic program. And you can customise the way the reference list is presented, depending on your requirements.

Bibliographic software programs are like database programs but more specialised. A general database program won't work well because the records that you are storing have a different format according to whether the source was a monograph, a chapter in an edited collection, a journal article or some other kind of source, such as a web document. Database programs are designed on the principle that all the records in a file (the complete set of records) should have the same structure, for example: customer's name, followed by customer's address, followed by customer's account. Bibliographic references are not like this; they have different formats according to the type of publication each reference is. If you do choose to invest in bibliographic software, be certain to keep a backup (or two) of your files. Losing them would be devastating.

We think that using a computer program to hold records of what you have read is more efficient than using a card system but, whatever method you use, the principles are the same. You want a record of the bibliographic details, some information about the subject matter, and a way of retrieving these details and this information after you have made the records. Whichever system you use, your bibliography files will help you compile the list of references for your present essay and they will also serve as a source of information for future assignments. They will grow as you move on from one task to the next. While you may change your mind about the ideas you developed in your first essay, your bibliography file will never be superseded. You can go on adding to the base that you are establishing now and it will be useful to you for the rest of your scholarly life.

Here is some practical advice about establishing a card system. Let's start with the 'author' card. On this you record all the bibliographic details, plus information about where you found the source in case you need to consult it again (though with good notes this may not be necessary), and a few words about the subject matter. A typical card might look like this:

SHORTER, EDWARD

1975 *The Making of the Modern Family* Basic Books, New York (U301.42 S5590)

(argues that the traditional family was constrained by local community and age peers, not just kin, but that these pressures were weakened by rise of capitalism and ideas about individualism, as in sentiment, sexuality, domesticity … see more detailed notes in folder on 'FAMILY')

Make up a separate one for every source you read. Do not put two (or more) sources on to the same author card. This may seem wasteful at first, but the advantage is that you can file each card in its box in alphabetical order by author, and keep on adding to the collection while still maintaining the alphabetical order.

Maybe, just as we find that we can sometimes fit all the notes we want on a source into the EndNote record, you may find that you can fit all the notes you need, page numbers and quotes included, on the 'author' card. Some people buy the largest kind to maximise the possibility of this. But if you have more notes than will fit, you can use the card to remind yourself of where you have put them as we have done in the example on Shorter. We have also added the library call number for Shorter's book, because that is where we found it. If it's your own copy write 'own copy' on the card. Later you may forget that you have the book. This may be hard to imagine when your academic library consists of three paperbacks but, in time, your collection will grow and your mental inventory of your possessions will become less effective. (It is frustrating to spend hours searching the library for an elusive book only to find that you had a copy on your own shelves all the time.)

For a while you will be able to manage with just a set of 'author' cards. But in time the collection will grow too big for you to do a quick search. The new essay is on 'Education, ideology and social class'. What do you already have on social class? On the socialisation of children? On educational institutions? On ideology? You don't know immediately and it will take a while to find out. At this stage you are going to need the second set of cards and the second box and a spare afternoon to establish the subject cards. The exact subject headings you will use depend on the content of the subjects you are taking and your own interests. But the way in which they are set out is simple. A subject card for 'ideology' is shown below.

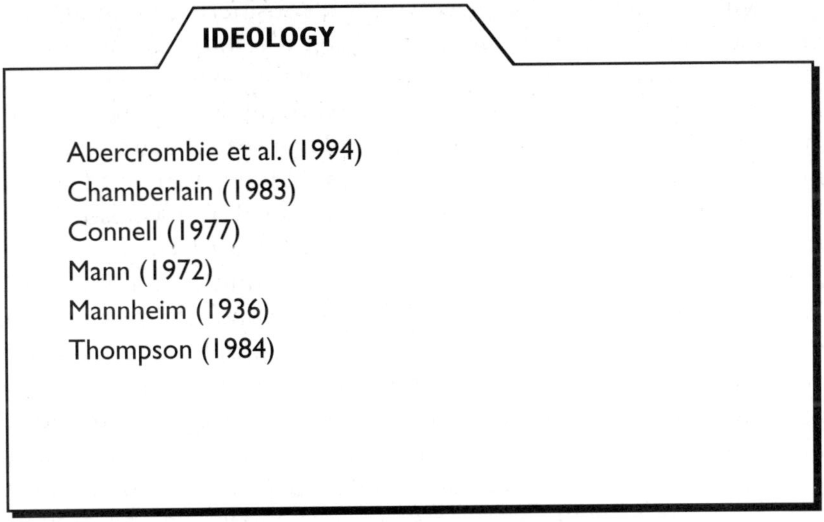

IDEOLOGY

Abercrombie et al. (1994)
Chamberlain (1983)
Connell (1977)
Mann (1972)
Mannheim (1936)
Thompson (1984)

With bibliographic software you just ask the program to search for the word 'ideology' and, in a second, the program will have assembled for you all of the references in your collection in which the word 'ideology' is mentioned either in the bibliographic details or in the notes you have added. You could repeat this for 'class', 'education' and 'socialisation', or you could ask the program to select only works that mentioned both 'class' and 'education', or 'class' and 'ideology'.

Whichever system you use, good bibliographical records are an investment for the future. They allow you to accumulate your own personal stock of knowledge in a systematic fashion and they reduce the number of occasions when you have to re-read a source. If the first occasion involved 'serious' reading, rather than a quick hunt for facts, this means a considerable saving of time.

Speed reading and serious reading

There are at least three ways of reading: a quick search for facts, names or dates; speed reading; and a thorough immersion in an author's themes and ideas. The quick search is more to do with looking things up than with either speed reading or serious reading. Serious reading takes effort and commitment but speed reading helps you minimise the risk of wasting time on an author who is not relevant to your topic, or not as useful, profound, or stimulating as the next one might have been if only you'd known about it. Obviously, your subject reading list provides hints about where you should make the heaviest investment of time, but speed reading can help you to make up your own mind. It is never a substitute for serious reading but it is a useful way of deciding whether a work merits serious reading.

We will assume that the piece you are considering is an article or a chapter (though, with modifications, speed reading techniques will work for books as well). How do you set about this swift reconnaissance? There may be an 'abstract', a short paragraph in which authors summarise their ideas. If there is, read it. Then read the first paragraph and the last paragraph. These together should give you an idea of the author's theme and the way in which it is handled. It may also give you an idea of the conclusion. Is the work on your topic? The first and last paragraphs should tell you. If the answer is 'definitely not' put it aside and try elsewhere. If it's 'yes' or 'maybe' try 'reading' the piece through by reading only the first sentence of each paragraph. This should give you an even clearer idea of the author's drift. (It can also provide you with some clues about writing. First paragraphs usually introduce the author's argument while last ones sum it up. In between, each paragraph represents one idea, or set of closely related ideas, and the first sentence of the paragraph usually introduces that idea and is often referred to as the *topic sentence*. See Chapter 7.)

Skimming in this way not only helps you decide whether to invest time in a particular work, it also makes that time more profitable. You will already have a rough idea of the author's theme before you start serious reading and so will be able to grasp the ideas involved more easily.

If you are deciding whether to read a whole book, begin with the table of contents. If that looks promising, 'speed read' the last chapter. One can usually make a decision on this basis and, if it's in the book's favour, begin with Chapter 1, speed reading it first and then reading it seriously. Treat all the chapters in the same way. Maybe you don't need to read all of them? It's not a crime if students only read parts of a book provided, of course, that they don't pretend that they have done so.

The critical appraisal

Serious reading is much more rewarding than speed reading. You have decided that an article or book deserves closer attention and now you can set about understanding what the author is saying. Many authors are keen to tell you about their ideas and you can absorb their message fairly easily. Others have not put much effort into communicating so you, as the reader, have to work harder. Whether the reading is a pleasure or a labour, you should keep at it until you understand and, if the work was really worth your serious attention, you should push yourself further and arrive at your own critical appraisal of the author's theme. You are not merely going to read, mentally summarise, and understand an article or book. You are going to evaluate it, to read it critically.

What does this mean? The principle here is the same as with the evaluative essays discussed in Chapter 2. Ask yourself three questions:

- What is this author's argument (theory, theme, point of view)?
- Am I convinced by it?
- If yes, why? (Or if no, why not?)

Of course you may be partly convinced by some aspects of the argument and partly unconvinced by others, but you should be able to explain this too. When you know your answers to these three questions you will have produced a critical appraisal of an author's work.

This may sound like a simple set of rules, but students often find them hard to follow. Perhaps the author is so hard to understand that you are not sure you know exactly what the argument is? In this case you have to suspend judgement. Make a note telling yourself that this is your conclusion. Maybe later on it will seem much clearer and, in the meantime, you can ask tutors and fellow students to help. Remember this is one of the many purposes of tutorials. Never feel that your inability to understand is a mark of intellectual failure. You have won a place at your university. This means that you have the ability to undertake the course you have enrolled in. You have also made a serious attempt to understand a piece of set reading. So far, on your own, you are stuck. Be brave enough to say so.

There are not many absolute certainties in this book but here, based on many years of teaching experience, we can offer you one. Lecturers and tutors cannot always guess beforehand which readings students will have difficulty with but, if one student in a group of ten or more has had trouble with a piece, at least a third of the others will have had difficulty too, if not the whole group. (However, if everyone is scared to say so, it's just possible that no one will find out and that no one, tutors included, will learn.)

Saying 'I don't understand' can take courage, especially in an unfamiliar setting, but by saying it you are making a valuable contribution to the intellectual climate of your class. It often seems easier to bluff it out and pretend that we know what's going on but, if large numbers of people are bluffing and keeping quiet, education stops. Worse still, if some students are tossing a few bits of jargon into the conversation to maintain a cool, superior image and conceal their fright, learning and understanding can freeze to death. So ask. Asking will provide an answer to your own particular problem and it will help ensure a warm and open intellectual climate for resolving problems next time.

When you have understood you can move on to the next two questions. Keep your answers with your notes (in brackets, italics, or green ink – whatever system you've devised). Be honest. These are your own notes to yourself and they are not set in concrete. Next year you may know more and your opinion may change. But you know now in your heart of hearts what you really think today. These are your own reactions to an author. You can draw on them in tutorial discussions if you want to or just brood over them for a while. Maybe you will polish them a little for your essay or maybe you won't use them right now.

But whatever use you make of your responses to questions two and three, make sure you do provide them for yourself.

Writing down the full bibliographic details of your sources, labelling them by subject, noting the contents, and adding your own stamp of approval or disapproval provides a certain feeling of mastery. The ocean of knowledge is not too big after all. You do not have to be overwhelmed by it. You have the means to stay afloat and chart your way through to the islands, getting more and more efficient all the time. 'But,' you say, 'it all seems rather dull. The ocean may be vast, but all that reading, note-taking, filing and cross-referencing sounds more like swimming a hundred laps in an indoor pool than gliding through foreign seas to strange, undiscovered places.' We agree. So read on.

Activities

1. Go to your library (or its web page) and locate the library catalogue. See if you can find the call number for one of your assigned books.
2. Visit the library's online databases. Do a keyword search for two words, such as 'green politics', and see what happens. What kinds of documents did your search yield? Try changing the way you entered the search terms, perhaps changing their order. Were the results different?
3. Find out whether your library gives students access to bibliographic software and, if they do, which sort they recommend.

4. Do a speed reading of one of your assigned readings. How effective was it? Now do a thorough reading of the same assigned reading. Take notes on it.

5. Construct a bibliographic filing system, either using cards or using bibliographic software. Enter the source you read in activity 4.

Chapter 4

The essay – structuring an argument

Objectives

➤ To learn what it means to structure an argument

➤ To learn how to approach developing and structuring an argument

Outline

➤ Evidence

➤ Arguing

➤ Developing your argument

➤ The conclusion

➤ The introduction

Sometimes, especially when a few heavy waves have crashed over their heads and the dark shapes of panic and despair are circling up from below, students think a particularly sad and depressing thought. It goes like this: 'Nobody cares about what you think at university. They just want you to read piles of books and repeat what the authors say.' Not only is this thought so boring and discouraging it would make you weep, it is wrong. Your teachers do care about your opinion, and they do want you to tell them about it, but – and this is the catch – it has to be your informed opinion grounded in the evidence. Every time you write a critical appraisal of a book or theory, or offer an explanation for some aspect of social reality, you are putting forward an opinion, but it must be an opinion tested and refined against objectively available evidence.

Evidence

What counts as evidence? All sorts of things. For example, the results of social surveys, government statistics, historical events, published biographies and letters are all evidence. But when you are looking at a piece of evidence, ask yourself: What sort of evidence is it? Is what you have read simply an author's personal judgement, or does it have some firmer basis? Whether or not a source counts as evidence depends on your purposes. An unsubstantiated assertion that Australia is suffering from 'moral decay' tells us little about the quality of social life in Australia, but it does tell us something about the author's state of mind. It is useful evidence if you want to document his or her thinking; if you want to document social change in Australia, it is not. Some students tend to 'argue from authority', tacitly assuming that if great and important personages have written something it must be true. Be sceptical of the 'authorities'; ask them for their evidence.

Some sources describe whole populations, others describe small groups or individuals. Whether this matters depends on the work you want them to do. Evidence that cultural conflict is making one migrant schoolgirl unhappy is valid evidence about her state of mind for someone writing her biography. But if they were to use it to document a claim that all (or most) migrant schoolgirls were unhappy they would be generalising from insufficient data. The crucial questions to ask about evidence are these:

- Is it valid and reliable evidence for the point I am trying to document?
- Can other people get access to it and check that I have used it properly?

In Chapter 5 we give you a set of rules for describing where your evidence comes from. It's important to follow them because, when you are careful to say where your evidence comes from, you allow other people to go and look at it themselves, to check whether it is indeed relevant to the point you are making, and to see whether you have got the story right. Objectively available evidence is evidence that other people can check; the phrase *objectively available* means no more than this.

Be careful about using facts that other people can't check as evidence. Radio and television programs are not very useful evidence because it's hard for other people to get access to recordings though, if there is a transcript on the web, you could refer to it. You should also avoid quoting from lecture notes. Go to the material the lecturer was drawing on and refer to it directly.

What about your own experience? Does that count as evidence? Of course it is real. To you it is more real than anything else. The problem is that other people are not able to check what you say about it. Use your own experience as evidence if you want to, but use it sparingly and in an illustrative way, and with other evidence as well. Lecturers and tutors do want to know about your experience; they *are* interested and it *does* matter, but you can't use it to support an argument all by itself, unless you are writing your autobiography.

Your experience, your unique point of view, may be what attracted you to study subjects in the social sciences in the first place; it can go on to fire your interest in certain topics, drive you to find explanations that work and challenge you, when you have done that, to strike out for the next island. Your desire to make sense of the world and your own place in it may be the point of the whole enterprise. You don't have to study sociology or politics or economic history in order to understand your world. You can explore it through literature, or express your response to it through art, dance, or music. But if you want to discuss your world in a way that other social scientists can understand and accept, you have to use the method of the reasoned argument grounded in objectively available evidence.

Arguing

We have talked about evidence. What about arguing? How, in practice, do you go about expressing your opinion when you write an essay? All you need to do is to be logical and to answer the question but, stated like that, the advice seems abrupt and unfriendly. Perhaps you'd find it more helpful if we gave you a couple of illustrations. Here we will work through an example of how to approach a question that asks you to explain an aspect of social life, while Appendix 1 contains a theoretical essay. This is provided both to illustrate the numbered footnote method of referencing – see Chapter 5 – and as a practical example of one student's finished product.

Let us imagine that your essay topic asks you to 'Explain changes in fertility in Australia since 1965'. How do you make a start? Don't reach for your pen and begin like this:

> I think people are having smaller families today because they are selfish and immature. People who are not prepared to have children should not be allowed to get married …

There are two things wrong with this approach and neither of them are to do with the fact that it expresses strong opinions. First, no evidence about the alleged selfishness and immaturity is presented and, second, the author is marching briskly away from the question, which asked for an *explanation*, and is heading off into another realm altogether (which we might call 'policy recommendation').

What would be a logical way of tackling the question? First of all you could gather material about changes in fertility and then start to organise it. Ask yourself, what exactly has happened? This will mean asking questions like: Are all families getting smaller, or are people who do have children having much the same number as their parents did, but a larger proportion are remaining childless? Are more women now having children outside of formal marriage? Are more children being born into de facto relationships? Are more women without partners having children? And so on.

What you are doing here is trying to pull together a picture of what has happened that is as neat and tidy and manageable as possible. You are organising the *evidence* about the changes you are interested in. When you have done this you will find that you have a draft form of a section of your essay written. Give it a heading. Maybe you could call it:

The nature of changes in fertility in Australia since 1965

You could find it helpful to divide the material up further. Perhaps a couple of sub-headings would be useful, for example:

Changes in nuptial fertility

Changes in ex-nuptial fertility

Use headings and subheadings. They help you to organise your material and to think about it more clearly, and they also help readers to see where they are in your argument.

If the question had asked you to describe changes in fertility you would work on improving and expanding this part of your draft, but in this case you have been asked to explain the changes. You went to the trouble of mapping them out because you needed to know what had happened before you could know whether a particular explanation was logical or not. For example, if some people were still having lots of children while others were having none, an explanation such as 'modern living is making everyone unhealthy and sub-fertile' would not be very convincing. No matter how much evidence an author brought forward about 'unhealthiness' you would reply 'but it doesn't fit the facts'; that is, 'this theory does not provide a logical explanation for the pattern of fertility I have discovered.'

Developing your argument

How are you going to tackle your next section, the section on explanation? You almost certainly had some ideas about the causes of changes in fertility before you began reading for your essay, and more of them flashed in and out of your mind while you were reading and while you were organising the first section. We all live in society and we all have ideas about how it works. Write your ideas down before they get away. But what about the books and articles you read? What sorts of ideas did other people have?

You have probably collected quite a few explanations in your reading; some of them compatible with each other, others not. There are theories about the economic costs and benefits of children to parents, theories about changes in the role of women and in the emotional quality of family life, theories about the influence of zero population growth and conservation ideologies, theories about the effect of changes in contraception, theories about the effects of housing costs and of women's growing participation in the labour force. Think about them. What sort of evidence have the writers relied on, and do their theories provide a logically convincing explanation for the pattern of change in fertility that you have discovered?

Now go back to that crumpled piece of paper (or neatly labelled initial computer file) where you recorded your own explanations. Have you changed your mind? Yes? No? Partly? Write down what happened and why.

By this time you will have a rough draft of your next section, perhaps on different pieces of paper, perhaps on your computer. In either case it will be starting to look like a section of an essay. You will need a new heading:

Explanations for changes in fertility since 1965

How are you going to organise this section? Perhaps you could begin like this:

> Explanations for changes in fertility seem to fall into two (or three, or four...) main categories. First, there are theories that focus on changes occurring outside the immediate circle of family life, for example, economic changes and changes in the law, and second, ...

Would more sub-headings be useful? Probably. For instance:

> The impact of economic recessions
> Access to effective contraception
> Women's increased work-force participation
> Changes in the marriage rate
> (and so on)

Where are you and your opinions in all this? You are there all the time. You are making judgements as you organise the material. (Why does this author go into this box? Well, she goes there because she takes the view that …) And you are there when you evaluate what your authors say.

Let us imagine that you have been reading an author who argues that the decline in births in the early 1970s was due to the spread of materialism, and of zero population growth ideology. You might write:

> This does not seem plausible to me. First, it assumes that people are becoming both more selfish (materialistic) and more altruistic (concerned with the world's population problems) at the same time. This is not logical. Second, it is not supported by the evidence. For example, Lyn Richards writes that many of the people she interviewed in the mid-1970s were opposed to the zero population growth movement and resented being told by outsiders how many children they should have (Richards, 1978: 229–230).

This is your opinion, but you have given your reasons for it so that other people can see whether it is fair and sensible or not.

The conclusion

You are there most of all when you write your conclusion. Of course, the conclusion will have been at the back of your mind all along. Remember what you did when you went back to your initial ideas? You either changed them, or you hung on to them, but you had reasons for this. If other authors seemed to have good explanations well grounded in the evidence, they influenced you. If they were muddled or had little evidence, you may have decided to disregard them. You knew why you were doing this and you defended your opinion in the language of reason and evidence.

You may have begun your essay with a strong opinion, or with only a scattering of ideas, but as you read and thought this changed. The scattered ideas became more organised and coherent, the strong opinion altered – perhaps a little, perhaps a lot. It has, as it were, been tried in the fire and it is the better and more convincing for it. It is an opinion well grounded in the evidence; it has developed into a reasoned argument.

Make sure that your conclusion pulls together the strands of your argument into a synopsis or summary. In effect, what you are doing here is telling your reader what happened to your ideas as they went through the fire. Perhaps you will point out how they changed. Perhaps you will show how they became more logical as you thought about them in mental debate with other authors, and as you forced them to confront the evidence you found. But your opinion may still have weaknesses. Explain these too. Almost certainly the perfect explanation has not been constructed. (This is one of the reasons why there are many ways to answer a given question and to do it well.) But your explanation is still the best you have been able to make.

The introduction

And then, last of all, go back and write the introduction. It is hard to write an introduction first because you almost certainly will not know how you are going to organise your thoughts and your material until you have tried. Here you can say why the topic is worth studying, briefly tell your reader how you are going to approach it, and define the concepts you are going to use.

Chapter 7 provides more help with writing, finding a good structure for your argument, accumulating ideas, and choosing the right words. What we have outlined here is a two-stage structure that works well with most questions about social reality:

- Describe the phenomenon you are interested in.
- Explain why it is like it is.

Many essays and research projects lend themselves to this pattern, but this guide is meant to be a life belt, not a straitjacket. You will probably be able to think of other ways of approaching topics, ways that interest you and which provide an appropriate answer to the question. Use your imagination. Throw the life belt away. But you must keep one part of it forever, the little navigation device (just to the left of the whistle for calling for help and the torch that lights up when in contact with water). The navigation device, when you look at it closely, is not a compass at all. It is a disc with two words on it, *logic* and *evidence*. Keep it and you will be all right.

Activity

1. Select one or two journal articles and first identify the author or authors' argument. Summarise it in 100 words or less.
2. Second, using the same article or articles, identify the kinds of evidence used. List them.
3. Third, decide whether you find the argument convincing and write down why you are or are not convinced.

Chapter 5

Acknowledging Sources (Referencing)

Objectives

➤ To learn why you need to acknowledge your sources
➤ To learn the principles behind in-text referencing
➤ To learn the principles behind referencing systems in general
➤ To provide examples showing how to reference different types of sources

Outline

➤ Why, when and how
➤ The author/date system
➤ The references in your text
➤ The list of references (or bibliography)
➤ The numbered footnote system
➤ Plagiarism
➤ Fraud

Why, when and how

Why

Why do your teachers at university insist on referencing? There are two reasons. First, as Chapter 3 shows, you need to tell your readers where your evidence comes from so that they can check it for themselves and see if it is indeed valid and reliable evidence for the point you are making. This is the way knowledge cumulates, and therefore it is the path by which your informed opinion can become part of accepted scholarship. Instead of being something ephemeral, a personal point of view that others can easily dismiss (perhaps as emotional, biased, prejudiced, or having no basis in fact), your informed opinion becomes a statement about the social world that other scholars will be prepared to take seriously.

Second, you need to use references in order to make it quite clear which are your own ideas, and your own words, and which are borrowed from other people. If you do not do this you are in effect passing off other people's work as your own. Students who do this on purpose are guilty of a particular kind of fraud called *plagiarism*. (So that there is no chance of unpleasant misunderstandings, plagiarism is defined quite specifically at the end of this chapter.)

For these two reasons you need to learn the rules set out here very well and to follow them carefully.

When

When should you document your material by providing a reference? A good maxim is: 'when in doubt, do.' But the general rule is this: all quotes, direct and indirect, need a reference and so do all 'statements of fact' that are not absolutely common knowledge.

How

There are two main ways of giving references:
- the author/date system
- numbered footnotes.

The author/date system is also known as the *Harvard system* or the *in-text system*; it is rather more common in the social sciences than numbered footnotes. Unless you are working with a word-processor that puts footnotes in for you and renumbers them automatically when you make revisions, it is also easier to use. Because of this, we used to recommend it. But as more and more students use word-processors and bibliographic software, the advantages of the author/date system are becoming less evident. (In fact, bibliographic software will format your references in whatever style you specify.)

Here we will show you how to use both systems. Whichever method your subject wants you to adopt, you will certainly be reading some sources that use the other one. Also, students often find that different subjects in the same faculty have different requirements; in one they must use the author/date system and in the other numbered footnotes. So you may have to come to terms with both. (First year can have its difficulties. We have every sympathy for the student who said, 'Who is this Ibid? He certainly wrote a lot.')

We will begin with the author/date system because it is still the method that social science students are most likely to be asked to use. We will describe it in some detail. The numbered footnote system will be illustrated by giving you a piece of prose documented in this way so you can see how it is done. It will be discussed briefly, but you can observe the details for yourself. (The piece of prose is the theory essay we promised you earlier; it is reproduced in Appendix 1.)

Though the setting-out varies, the principles behind the two methods are same. These include the general principle of providing readers with all the information about a source that they will need if they are to find it, and the specific principles of how to refer to direct quotes, indirect quotes, quotes within quotes, and the like.

The author/date system

With the author/date system all references to books, articles and other sources must be identified at the appropriate point in the text by putting in brackets the surname of the author, year of publication and page number or numbers, as in (Mills, 1970: 9–14). The in-text reference, also called a citation, is complemented by a list of sources, complete with full bibliographic details, at the end of the essay (or article, or book). There readers can look up 'Mills, 1970' and find all the information they need to locate the actual book or article you have read.

Quotes, verbatim or paraphrased, need a page number, as does any reference to specific research findings. If your source has no named author, list it by either the organisation that produced it or by its title. In rare cases you may be referring to a book or article as a whole and there is no need to give page numbers, but when specific material is being used you should give page numbers so that readers can check the accuracy of your statements. When in doubt about adding page numbers, put them in. See example 14 below.

The rules of the method rest on two principles: brevity and adequacy. The reference in your text should be as brief and unobtrusive as possible, but it must contain enough information to allow readers to trace the source easily in your final list of references. You can use footnotes to expand a point in your essay but try to keep this to a minimum.

Never mix the two systems of referencing. For example, if you are using the author/date system you might need a footnote to explain how a total fertility rate is calculated but you would not use one for documenting your sources. Documentation appears in your text.

The references in your text

The following examples show how the author/date system allows you to differentiate between the various ways in which you have used the works you have consulted.

1. *An indirect quote*

This example shows the acknowledgement of an indirect quote:

> Mills argues that if we think about individual lives and individual problems in the broader context of political, economic and social change we will understand them more clearly (1970: 9–14). By this he means …

Here you have expressed the author's ideas in your own words. The name 'Mills' does not appear in the brackets because it is quite clear from the context whom you are referring to. Even though it is an indirect quote, we have provided page numbers. Sceptical readers should be able to trace your source with the minimum of effort. If the page numbers were not there they might have to read the whole book to see if you had paraphrased the author's ideas in a reasonable way. The pages are indicated as 9–14, meaning that the idea is developed over the space of these six pages. If the reference were to read (1970: 9, 14) this would mean that the idea was developed only on pages number 9 and 14. See example 12 below.

Be sure to note the position of the full stop. It comes after the brackets. We have spent many a sleepless night fretting about the inability of some students to perceive the importance of this. If the full stop came before the brackets rather than after, a reader would think that the reference was documenting the next sentence rather than the one you had just finished.

Some academic disciplines don't include page numbers for indirect quotes. However, most lecturers will appreciate their inclusion because it makes checking sources much easier. If in doubt, ask your lecturer what he or she would prefer.

2   *A direct quote*

This example shows the acknowledgement of the direct quote:

> Hardin argues that, 'trustworthiness is *not* a commodity, even though perceived trustworthiness (that is, reputation) is' (2001: 22, emphasis in the original).

This acknowledges *a direct quote*. The format is the same as in the first example. Sometimes people split the reference: 'Hardin (2001) writes that "trustworthiness is *not* a commodity, even though perceived trustworthiness (that is, reputation) is" (p.22).' Avoid this. Remember, the reference in your text should be as brief and unobtrusive as possible. Split references interrupt the reader twice rather than just once.

Also notice that that we have said that the italics were in the original document by Hardin. If we had added the italics ourselves, in order to emphasise a particular word, we would have said that the emphasis had been added.

Here is another example of a direct quote:

> Sociologist Barbara Risman suggests: 'Arlie Hochschild's theoretical insights have shaped the sociological imagination of the late 20th century' (2005: 128).

3   *Direct quotes longer than three lines*

Direct quotes longer than three lines should be indented. Do not use quotation marks and, if you are double spacing, switch to single spacing. For example:

In the *Communist Manifesto,* Marx and Engels point to class differences in family relationships:

> On what foundation is the present family, the bourgeois family, based? On capital, on private gain. In its completely developed form this family exists only among the bourgeoisie. But this state of things finds its complement in the practical absence of the family among the proletarians, and in public prostitution. (Marx & Engels, 1952: 68)

If this insight held true in the nineteenth century, can it help us to understand patterns of family formation today?

Here the full stop can go before the in-text reference because, thanks to the indentation, there is no confusion about the piece of prose it refers to. (Maybe this difference between indented and unindented quotes explains students' confusion?) Though one would be able to guess the names of the authors from the text, they are repeated in the citation because the quotation is so long readers might forget and feel that they had to glance back to find them.

Use direct quotes sparingly. If an essay is a string of direct quotes it will not read well. Sometimes students who have laboured to patch together a collection of all the best bits and pieces of direct quotes they can find are disappointed to be told that they are guilty of 'lazy writing'. What their tutor means is that they haven't worked on developing their own argument, their own informed opinion.

There are two occasions when long direct quotes are appropriate: when the author has expressed an idea extremely well; and when you believe the author is wrong. In the latter case it's only fair to allow the author to put their case in their own words before you move in to attack. These instances apart, try to use example 1 more than 2 or 3, putting the ideas into your own words and giving the appropriate reference.

When you paraphrase, it is important to make it quite clear which are your ideas and which are borrowed. Beginning your paraphrase by mentioning the author's name and ending with the page references accomplishes this. See example 1.

4   *A quote from a chapter in an edited collection of readings*

The following example is a direct quote taken from a chapter in an edited collection of readings. When quoting (both directly and indirectly) from edited collections, you must cite the name of the person who actually wrote the chapter you are referring to, not the name of the editor or editors. This type of reference seems to cause students trouble. Do check carefully to see how a source of this kind is entered in the section on **The list of references (or bibliography)** and compare it with example 5, a quote within a quote. Beginners often get these two kinds of sources muddled.

> The idea of relativism, the idea that we may have no access to standards of absolute truth or of good behaviour, has long been discussed by social theorists. But postmodernist philosophers approach relativism from a different perspective. Like much else in postmodern thought, their view of relativism comes from their view of language, and its history can be traced through structuralism and deconstructionism (see Parker, 1992: 82). Both of these movements have been much concerned with language, either as an object of study in its own right or as a metaphor shedding light on other aspects of culture.

The chapter by Ian Parker appears in a collection of essays edited by Doherty, Graham and Malek. Parker is the author and both the in-text citation and the full bibliographic details should be entered under his name, not those of the editors. Imagine you have written a prize-winning essay in a national competition. There are nine other prize-winners and all the essays are going to be collected into one volume by the president of the Australian Sociological Association and published as an inspiration to other students. The president of the Sociological Association will be the editor, but you will be the author. This distinction will be important to you. People who read future books and articles in which your essay is referred to will also want to be sure that it is indeed your essay that is under discussion, not that of the winner from Townsville or Mildura or Port Hedland.

Note that the citation of Parker's work must include his name, because this has not been mentioned in the text, and also that it says '*see* Parker...' When do you insert 'see' in the citation and when do you leave it out? It's a matter of judgement. With a direct quote you would not use 'see'. The author's words have been presented to speak for themselves. But if you think that your paraphrase, rather than being a direct re-statement of the author's words, either builds on them a little, or is a rather loose translation, or that it refers to the author as one among a number of possible examples, as is the case above, it can be fairer to the author to put in the 'see'. To leave it out could imply either that the paraphrase or summary is quite direct, as it is in example 1, or that Parker was the only person to have written in this way. But the matter is not serious; it's a question of your judgement.

5 *A quote within a quote*

Chapters in edited collections stand by themselves as the independent work of one author (or group of authors working as a team). They are very different from *quotes within quotes*. The following passage contains two references. The first is to a journal article. Journal articles will be discussed further under example 6. But the second is a reference to a quote within a quote. It shows you how to refer to material that you have not read yourself but which you have read about in someone else's work.

> Arthur Calwell was Australia's first Minister for Immigration in the Chifley Government of the immediate post-war years. He was impressed by the American image of the cultural 'melting pot' and considered that Australia had much to gain from non-British, European migrants as well as from Britons (Markus, 1984: 28–29). He established a fact-finding committee late in 1945. This committee recommended that: 'A national publicity campaign should be launched conditioning the Australian citizen for the arrival of migrants, assuring

him that the new citizen will MAKE jobs not TAKE them'
(quoted in Calwell, 1972: 100, emphasis in the original).

In principle, if you find an interesting reference to a source in
someone else's work and you want to use it, you should go to that
source and read it for yourself. But sometimes, especially if the original
is unpublished or hard to find, you have to opt for second best. The
author of this passage has done this with the recommendations of
Calwell's fact-finding committee. The quoted material was not written
by Calwell, it was written by the committee and quoted by him. The
citation therefore reads, not (Calwell, 1972: 100), but (quoted in
Calwell, 1972: 100). Also note that we have added 'emphasis in the
original' to the end of our citation. This is so that the reader will
know that we have not capitalised those words ourselves – they were
originally that way.

6 Acknowledging something that has been cited by another author

Sometimes you will find that one of your references has itself referred
to another author's idea, and it is this idea that you would like to use
for your essay. However, your reference does not quote this author;
the author you have read has paraphrased the other person's idea.
As we noted in example 5, you really should look up the work being
referred to yourself. The paraphrasing done by your reference might
not accurately reflect the original author's intent, or may be missing
some nuances.

But what do you do if that other author's publication is not available?
You can still refer to the work, but your in-text reference will need to
reflect that you did not actually read it yourself. For example:

According to Hall, the media both reflect and shape reality
(cited in Farquharson, 1999: 178).

As you can see from the example, you should acknowledge the
source of your idea (in this case, Hall), but your in-text reference needs
to refer to the item you actually read, which in this case was the article
by Farquharson and it is Farquharson (1999) who will appear in your
list of references, not Hall. You cannot include references to items on
another author's reference list unless you have read them yourself.

Here is another example:

It has been asserted that: 'the values of science have long been
perceived to be in conflict with those of religion' (Fulljames
cited in Critchley & Turney, 2004: 7).

This example includes a direct quote from a journal article by
Critchley and Turney. The person who argues this about the values
of science and religion is Fulljames, but the people who stated the

argument in this way (who paraphrased Fulljames's argument) were Critchley and Turney.

7   *A statement of fact*

Let's continue the theme of the passage in example 5, giving another example of a quotation from a journal article, this time documenting *a statement of fact*.

> While many people have questioned the image of the 'melting pot', statistics show a fair degree of intermarriage between people of different ethnic backgrounds in Australia. In 1988, people of solely 'Anglo-Celtic' origin made up 48 per cent of the country's population, 'non-Anglo-Celts' about 22 per cent, and a mixture between 'Anglo-Celts' and 'non-Anglo-Celts' accounted for the remaining 30 per cent (Price, 1993: 8).

Remember, all statements of fact that are not absolutely common knowledge need a reference. The fact that this one comes, not from a monograph or from a chapter in an edited collection, but from a journal article is not apparent here in the in-text citation. But it will be apparent in the list of references that follows.

8   *A source with more than two authors*

What if a source has more than two authors? If there are only two authors you provide the names of both, as in (Marx & Engels, 1952: 68) in example 3 above. With three (or more) you give the name of the first author followed by the phrase 'et al.', which is an abbreviation of a Latin expression, *et alia* (and others). This is used because it is shorter than 'and others'. As the following example shows, you can also use it in the text itself.

> What is postmodernism? Some postmodernists prefer not to answer this question. While Graham et al. do provide some definitions they also suggest that it might be better simply to offer postmodernist writing, unencumbered with explanations. In this way readers could directly experience 'the variety, the fragmentation, the differences and perhaps the confusions which have become as much features of the literature on postmodernism as they are said to be of postmodernism itself' (Graham et al., 1992: 1).

There is a convention that words taken from a foreign language should be put in italics, or underlined. (This at least can save readers from the fruitless task of looking them up in an English language dictionary.) Consequently some people put 'et al.' in italics. We have not done so here because 'et al.' is widely used and we don't want to make the text look too cluttered. But it's optional. The only rule in such cases is 'be consistent'; if you use italics for 'et al.' in one instance, make sure you use them in the next instance.

9 *More than one work by the same author*

Sometimes you may need to refer to two or more works written by the same author in the same year. When this happens, you give each item a letter. Usually you list them in the order they appear in your text: the first work you refer to is listed as 'a', the second 'b', and so on. In the following example there are two works by Garrett Hardin both published in 1993. They have been labelled 'a' and 'b'.

> Garrett Hardin writes that 'demographers' projections must be the basic data of all political prophecy' (1993a: 219). He also argues that, just as natural scientists have accepted that we live in a world bound by natural limits, so should economists. But he claims economists insist that the burden of proof lies with the ecologists; it is for ecologists to demonstrate that there are indeed limits to growth. 'Shifting the burden of proof is tactically shrewd: but would economists agree that the burden of proof must be placed on the axiom, "There's no such thing as a free lunch"?' (1993b: 44).

This example also shows you how to punctuate a quote within a quote. If different authors have the same surname, use their initials in the in-text citation, even if the dates for their work are different.

10 *Electronic documents*

Increasingly, we are finding sources for academic essays online. Some online sources can be referred to in a similar fashion to sources published elsewhere: by the author's surname, the year, and the page number that you are referring to. But some online sources cannot be referred to in this way because there is no apparent author, date of publication or page number. What do you do then?

There tend to be two types of electronic document. The first type is an electronic copy of a printed publication. These documents, usually PDF files, can be treated in the same way as the publication itself.

PDF stands for Portable Document Format. Documents in PDF style keep their original formatting. Downloading a PDF is essentially the same as taking a photocopy from a journal in the library. So if you download an academic journal article from an academic database, for example, your in-text citation would refer to it using the author's surname, year and page number. There is no need to mention that the version you have was accessed from an online source.

However, most online documents, including many from academic journals, are not electronic copies of printed documents. These are usually individual web pages in HTML format (HyperText Markup Language, the language used on the World Wide Web). They do not contain page numbers. They often also don't contain the names of the authors of the documents or the year when they were published. In fact, printouts from web pages in HTML format will vary depending on the type of browser you use. How should you reference these in your text?

If you can locate an author, you should refer to the documents by the author's surname. If there is no author, you can refer to the document by its title (for example: 'Glossary of Jamaican Reggae-Rasta words, expressions and slang'), or by the organisation that is responsible for it (for example: DEST). If there is no year, you should use the term 'n.d.', which stands for 'no date': ('Glossary of Jamaican Reggae-Rasta words, expressions and slang', n.d.) or (DEST, n.d.). (DEST is an acronym for Department of Employment, Science and Training. The entry in your list of references will make this clear. See the discussion of PIC in section 11 below.)

Page numbers are a bit trickier. Technically, web pages in HTML format are one-page long, no matter how many times you have to scroll down to reach the bottom. Since this is the case, and since different printouts may have different page numbering, some authorities argue that it is not appropriate to include page numbers with in-text references to web pages. We disagree. The principle of including page numbers exists so that your readers can easily look up your references for themselves. This is no different with online references. We suggest that you print out your electronic document and use the page numbers from your printout with your in-text reference. To tell the reader that the number is from a printout of a web page, and is therefore an approximation, put the number in square brackets.

> Although just 1% of girls were enrolled in engineering degree courses in 1970, 16% were enrolled in engineering courses in 1996 (Swords, n.d.: [1]).

> Just over half of Australian adults are now shareholders (White et al., 2004: [1]).

The square brackets show that the page number referred to is from your printout of a web page. Although your reader's printout may be a bit different in length to yours, your page number will provide him or her with much appreciated guidance regarding where to locate your quote or statement of fact.

Sometimes you might want to include a reference to an online discussion or forum. In this case the author would most likely use a pseudonym instead of their real name.

> A recent post to an online forum (badhairday, 2005: [1]) asked
> for advice about using Windows Media Player.

In this example, 'badhairday' is the pseudonym of the author. Since we do not know his or her real name, we must use the username.

Elists are email discussion lists. Individuals who subscribe to an elist receive messages posted to the list by email. Many elists are archived online and these can sometimes be used as sources for your essays. Like the example above, people often post messages to elists under their usernames.

> 'The Pew Internet Report on the Future of the Internet' was
> recently announced on the Association of Internet Researchers
> elist (J.J., 2005).

The author's name is his or her online username (J.J.), and there is no page number because author's post to the list was the press release announcing the Pew Internet Report on the Future of the Internet and only took up one page of printout.

For many online databases you have the option of choosing either HTML or PDF versions of the document you would like. If you have the choice, choose the PDF because it makes referencing simpler. PDFs should be treated like other web pages if they are not copies of documents published elsewhere; refer to them in the same way as you would HTML web pages.

11 *Government publications*

Students often worry about how to refer to government publications. Where an author's name is given, refer to him or her. If the work is presented as having been written by a committee, refer to it. If neither of these is possible, use the name of the government department that produced the work, or the title. Publications put out by the Australian Bureau of Statistics are usually referred to by their title. The first example given below is from an Australian Bureau of Statistics publication; the second is from a work prepared by a committee.

> There is a growing trend in Australia for couples to live together
> in de facto relationships. De facto couples in Australia tend
> to be younger, and less likely to have been legally married to

someone else before forming their current relationship, than older couples (*Australian Social Trends*, 2002: 47–49).

Because *Australian Social Trends* is not an author's name but the title of a book, it is set in italics or it is underlined.

The report, *Population Issues and Australia's Future*, suggests that Australia's immigration program could be halved from its 1991/92 level of 110 000 to a core of 55 000 and that such a program would lead to a population growing to 22 million in 2030 and then stabilising (Population Issues Committee, National Population Council, 1992: 109).

'Population Issues Committee, National Population Council' is rather a mouthful. If you needed to refer to this report more than once it is quite in order to use the initial letters of the committee that wrote it, rather than the full name, provided that you make it clear to your reader that you are going to do this. (Here you could use either 'PIC', or 'PIC, NPC'. It doesn't matter which, provided you are consistent and provided you repeat the letters in your list of references at the end of the essay.)

The conventional way of making it clear that you are switching from the name in full to using initials is to give the full name the first time you use it, followed by the initials in brackets. Then, for the rest of the essay, you can simply use the initials, as in the following example.

The Population Issues Committee of the National Population Council (PIC) argues that, while the government might have various reasons for wanting to add to this core figure of 55 000 immigrants, 'ecological integrity would be best served by no additional numbers' (1992: 110). But the force of this conclusion is undermined by the claim that a program of between 80 000 and 160 000 immigrants per year would not make much difference to 'average material living standards' (1992: 110). Its final recommendations simply state that Australia's population policy should 'understand that national ecological integrity and equity in funding of urban growth may be advanced by lower population growth' (PIC, 1992: 123).

12 *Several sources at once*

What should you do if you want to refer to a number of sources at the same time? This can be useful. For example you can strengthen a point by citing more than one source which has provided relevant evidence. Simply separate multiple citations by using semi-colons as we have done in the third sentence in the example below. And, if the evidence is scattered on a number of pages within the sources, you should provide these too.

> Because there is a dominant discourse of 'colour blindness' in the United States, it is taboo to discuss race there (Frankenberg, 1993: 14, 15, 142–148). Kendall (2000: 270) argues that this taboo, combined with the large numbers of whites online, 'enables whites to assume that other online participants are also white.' Social cleavages off-line, then, appear to be reproduced online (see Kendall, 2000: 259–60, 271; Nakamura, 2000: 15; Burkhalter, 1999: 62).

13 *Lecture notes*

How should you refer to lecture notes? The brief answer is that you should not. You should go to the material that the lecturer has been drawing on, read it, and refer to it directly. But perhaps the material comes from the lecturer's own research and is not, or is not yet, in print? Ask him or her about this. The conventional way of referring to such a source is (personal communication, Dr Jane Smith [substitute the name of your informant], followed by the date).

14 *Works as a whole*

Should you ever refer to a work as a whole without reference to page numbers? You will often find books and articles where the author has done this, and your tutor may expect you to do so too. However we recommend that, if not instructed otherwise, you should always include page numbers. Your work is being marked and the person marking it will want to be able to check your sources. (Besides, students are often held to higher standards than published authors.)

One instance where you might skip page references is in referring to a very brief research article, an article that is itself only two or three pages long. Many of the published works which appear to be leaving out page numbers are relying on sources of this kind. But if in doubt, include the page number in your reference. You have the page number in your notes and it's easy to share it with your reader.

Another category of material where reference is made to work as a whole is textbooks. When the authors of an introductory text write 'Shilling (1993) provides an interesting overview of the sociology of the body', they mean: 'It would be a good idea if you went away and read Shilling's book. All of it.' This is a reasonable suggestion for a teacher to make. We refer to some works as a whole here in this book; we want to draw your attention to authors who have written introductions to the social sciences, or to in-depth accounts of research methods and statistics, or to self-help books on grammar. When we are doing this we are, in effect, saying: 'If you want to know more about this topic, these books or articles provide a good place to start.' But when you are drawing on sources to construct an argument you don't want to be saying: 'The following five books support my position; please go and read them right through and then you will see that this is so.'

15 *Legal documents*

On occasion social science students find that they need to refer to a legal document. The legal documents you are most likely to need to refer to include Acts of Parliament (statutes) and Case Law. Acts of Parliament are referred to in your text by their short title, the year they were passed and their jurisdiction. The title of the Act is written in italics. Usually page numbers are not included with references to legal documents. Instead section (abbreviated 's'), subsection, and (where subsections are not numbered) paragraphs are included. In the following example the author is referring to section 7, subsection 1.

> In 2000 the Victorian Labor government passed legislation amending the *Tobacco Act* 1987 (Vic). Among other things, this legislation, the *Tobacco (Amendment) Act* 2000 (Vic), banned smoking in enclosed restaurants, cafes, some take-away shops and in dining areas within hotels and licensed premises. Smoking was also banned in non-eating areas within restaurants (such as bars), unless these areas were completely enclosed and away from the dining area (*Tobacco (Amendment) Act* 2000 (Vic) s 7(1)).

The Act referred to in the example above also contains further subsections. If we were referring to a subsection of the subsection, those numbers would go in subsequent sets of parentheses. See for example: (*Tobacco (Amendment) Act* 2000 (Vic) s 7(1),(2)(1)). This would referred the reader back to section 7, subsection 1 and subsection 2 paragraph 1.

Case Law is the body of law created through judges' written decisions in specific court cases. The cases are referred to by the parties' surnames (separated by a 'v' for versus). If there is more than one party only the first party is listed. The year can be either the year when the case was judged or the year when it was cited in a law report. The names of the parties should be in italics. An in-text reference to a case might look like this: (*Commonwealth v Tasmania* (1983) 158 CLR 1, 2). Here, the case was decided in 1983. It was reported in Volume 158 of *Commonwealth Law Reports* and the relevant pages are one and two.

16 *Altering direct quotes*

What do you do if you need to *alter direct quotes*? Sometimes you don't want to give a direct quote in full. It is permissible to leave out a phrase and you show you have done this by inserting an ellipsis (three dots) in place of the missing words.

> According to Levi, an institution becomes trustworthy when the processes that are in place for choosing its associates are geared to select 'agents ... so that they are competent, credible, and likely to act in the interests of those being asked to trust the institution' (Levi, 1998: 80).

The dots show that something has been left out. Or perhaps you may need to add something so that the quote makes sense within your context. You can do this by putting the added material within square brackets. This shows that the extra words are yours and not those of the authors.

> Kendall ultimately argues that, 'discussions of whiteness [in the online community] disavow identification with the very top of the dominance chain, yet ultimately leave intact the taken-for-granted workings of racial dominance found in American society' (2000: 270).

Without the addition of 'in the online community', the quote from Kendall would seem to apply to all of American society. In her article, however, it is clear that she is only discussing whiteness in one particular online community. For the quote to reflect her argument accurately you need to add this information.

What do you do if an author whom you want to quote directly has made a mistake? Perhaps there is a mistake in spelling or grammar or maybe a misquoted figure? If it is a direct quote don't correct the mistake. Instead, you put the word 'sic' which means 'thus' in square brackets after it. For example:

> Smith has many whimsical stories about his old car. He writes, 'It was always breaking down at odd moments. It was as if it had a mind of it's [sic] own' (2005:104).

This shows your reader that the mistake was in the original and has not been introduced by some carelessness on your part. This is a made-up reference. (The mistake with 'it's' is explained in Chapter 7.)

The list of references (or bibliography)

By now you will understand why, in Chapter 3, we emphasised the need to record details about authors, dates, and pages when you were reading. In your final list of references, which should appear on a separate page at the end of your essay, you will list your sources alphabetically by author's surname, showing the date clearly, and give all the other bibliographic details you have recorded. This page should be headed *References*. Sometimes it's called a 'bibliography' but the word *bibliography* also means a list of every existing work published on a particular topic. As your list is restricted to the works you have used directly in your text, it's more accurate to call it 'references'. The purpose of this list is to help readers who want to follow up the sources you used. Do not enter works that you have not referred to. Your in-text citations and your final list of references are the two halves of the same whole: a complete and scholarly system of documenting sources.

Put the list in alphabetical order and, when you are doing this, use the author's surname as the key word or, if more than one author is involved, the name of the first author. Put the surname first, followed by the initial or first name. If an individual author was not cited, as was the case here with the Population Issues Committee of the National Population Council and *Australian Social Trends,* list the source in your alphabetical list under the identifying word or phrase you used in your in-text reference, usually the organisation or the title of the document (for example, *Australian Social Trends*).

The 'full bibliographic details' described in Chapter 3 must be provided in the list. There is nothing arbitrary about this. The details are necessary if a reader is to be able to find your source in a bookshop, order it from the publisher, locate it in a library, or find it on the Internet. The bibliographic details can be thought of as your source's 'address'. With these details, a librarian (or bookseller) should be able to trace your source for any reader, even one on the other side of the world.

Here we give you the bibliographic details for the publications cited above in **The references in your text**, with some explanatory notes. Rather than putting them in alphabetical order, we've organised them by type. (To see what a list looks like, organised alphabetically and uncluttered by a series of explanatory notes, turn to the end of this book and have a look at ours.) Remember, there are three basic types of sources: books (monographs), chapters in edited collections, and articles in journals (serials). We have also discussed three other types: government publications, legal sources, and electronic sources. We have arranged this list into these three main categories plus the three minor ones to help you see how sources of each type are entered.

1 *Books (monographs)*

Calwell, A. (1972), *Be Just and Fear Not*, Lloyd O'Neil, Melbourne.

This work by Calwell is an example of a book (monograph) written by a single author. The year is the year that the book was published. The title is italicised. You also need to record the name of the publisher and the place where the book was published. You'll be able to find this information on the back of the title page.

With all monographs it is important to show which edition you are using. Most often a book comes out in only one edition, as is the case with Calwell (1972). But sometimes it can be substantially revised and reprinted. If this happens we talk of the first and second edition (or whatever number of the edition is involved) and you need to show which edition it is that you yourself have used. You do this by showing the correct date. (See Marx and Engels (1950) and Mills (1970) below.)

Lloyd O'Neil is the name of the publisher and Melbourne is the place of publication. Note that the place of publication is the town or city where the work was published, not the country. If you fear your reader may not know where Melbourne is, you can follow it with 'Australia', but the name of the country by itself is too imprecise. For example, there are thousands of publishers in the United States. If the book you are using was produced by a small publishing firm, a reader who was told only that it was published in the United States might still not be able to trace it. At the other end of the scale, a big publishing house might operate in a number of American cities. A keen reader who wanted to order a copy of such a book would lose time while the book shop tried to work out whether it was published by the Los Angeles or New York branch. You have the information on the town or city in front of you and this is the information that a reader or a librarian needs to locate another copy of the work that you have used.

> Hardin, G. (1993b), *Living Within Limits: Ecology, Economics, and Population Taboos*, Oxford University Press, New York.

This is another example of a monograph, with a single author. Books take more time to read than chapters or articles but they are simpler to enter. Remember, we used 'a' and 'b' in the in-text citation because we had two sources by Garrett Hardin published in 1993, and 'a' and 'b' must appear in the list of references as well so that readers can distinguish between them. This is also a first edition. (Journals and the articles in them only appear once, so the question of first and subsequent editions does not arise.)

> Marx, K., & Engels, F. (1952), *Manifesto of the Communist Party*, Progress Publishers, Moscow.

The *Manifesto of the Communist Party* is a monograph (in this case a fairly substantial pamphlet), that has been through many editions and many printings. The edition we quoted from was published in Moscow in 1952, but Marx and Engels originally wrote the work, in German, in 1848. Since then it has been reprinted frequently and translated into a number of languages. The authors themselves wrote new prefaces for some of these editions and Engels, after Marx's death, annotated the text in 1888 and 1890.

We have used the date '1952' not '1848' because the edition we quoted from was published in 1952. The page number we gave for our quotation is accurate for this edition; it may well not be accurate for another edition that used a different typeface or a different page size. This is why it is so important to specify the date of the edition you consulted so that others can check your use of the source. You don't have to say 'second edition' or 'twelfth edition'; indeed with a work like this it would be hard to know what number it actually was, and the information would not help a reader find the version we used. You do have to give the correct date and the correct publisher. This information allows the reader to track down a copy of your version. If it is necessary to your argument to make it clear that Marx and Engels originally produced the booklet in 1848, not 1952, say so in your text. You could put it like this: 'Writing in 1848, Marx and Engels claim that...'

Don't be confused by editions and printings. This edition of Marx and Engels was published in 1952, but has been reprinted many times. But these reprints were just re-runs of the 1952 edition and no significant changes were made. For your purposes reprints are irrelevant but new editions matter. Ignore the dates of reprints; pay close attention to the dates of editions. You will usually find information about the dates of editions, and reprints, on the reverse side of a book's title page.

Mills, C.W. (1970), *The Sociological Imagination*, Penguin, Harmondsworth.

This is another example of a monograph that has been through more than one edition (and more than one printing). On the back of the title page of our copy is the following information:

Penguin Books Ltd, Harmondsworth,
Middlesex, England
Penguin Books Australia Ltd, Ringwood,
Victoria, Australia
First published by Oxford University Press, New York, 1959
Published in Pelican Books 1970
Reprinted 1971

This tells us that, while the book first came out in 1959, the edition in front of us was published in 1970 and reprinted one year later. The date that we use is '1970' for the edition (not '1971' for the reprint). It also tells us that Penguin publishes in more than one place, and has various trade names ('imprints') for different types of books (in this case 'Pelican'). We cited the place listed first (here Harmondsworth not Ringwood), because publishers with a number of branches always put the branch where a particular book was published first in their list of offices that they provide inside the book. We also used the name of the publishing house, *Penguin*, rather than the imprint, *Pelican*, because this would be easier for a reader to trace. (Maybe everybody knows about 'Pelicans' but this may not be the case with a trade name used by a smaller publishing house. But we are getting into fine details here. To write 'Pelican' instead of 'Penguin' would not matter very much.)

These are also single-author, first edition, monographs:

Shilling, C. (1993), *The Body and Social Theory*, Sage, London.

Frankenberg, R. (1993), *The Social Construction of Whiteness: White Women, Race Matters*, University of Minnesota Press, Minneapolis.

2 Books (chapters in edited collections)

Here are two examples of chapters from edited collections:

Hardin, R. (2001), 'Conceptions and explanations of trust', in K. Cook, (Ed.), *Trust in Society, Vol. II*, Russell Sage Foundation, New York.

Graham, E., Doherty, J., & Malek, M. (1992), 'Introduction: the context and language of postmodernism', in J. Doherty, E. Graham and M. Malek (Eds), *Postmodernism and the Social Sciences*, Macmillan, London.

The chapters by Graham et al. above and Parker (1992) below are from the same book. But the Graham et al. chapter is particularly interesting because it is a chapter with multiple authors who, collectively, are also the editors of the book. When you can dash off both the in-text citation and the final entry for a piece like this, without missing a beat, you will know you have mastered the system.

Imagine that the president of the Australian Sociological Association has written an introductory chapter to that important volume where your prize winning essay has been published. The Graham et al. entry is just like this, except that there is more than one editor, and thus more than one author of the introductory chapter. List multiple authors, and multiple editors, in the order in which they appear in the published work.

The abbreviation for 'editors' is 'Eds', without a full stop, on the principle that if an abbreviation ends with the same final letter as the original word (like Mr and Mrs) you don't need a full stop. In contrast, the abbreviation for 'editor' is 'Ed.', with a full stop. If you write ed. with a small 'e' it usually means 'edition' as in 'first edition', 'second edition' and so on. Getting this muddled up is not a capital offence.

(Remember, you don't have to specify the number of the edition in your entry; you just need to get the date right.)

Here are four more chapters from edited collections. Look at them carefully. Whatever you do, remember the format!

> Burkhalter, B. (1999), 'Reading race online: discovering racial identity in Usenet discussion', in M.A. Smith and P. Kollock (Eds), *Communities in Cyberspace*, Routledge, London.
>
> Levi, M. (1998), 'A state of trust', in V. Braithwaite and M. Levi (Eds), *Trust and Governance*, Russell Sage Foundation, New York.
>
> Nakamura, L. (2000), '"Where do you want to go today?" Cybernetic tourism, the Internet, and transnationality', in B. Kolko, L. Nakamura and B. Rodman (Eds), *Race in Cyberspace*, Routledge, New York.
>
> Parker, I. (1992), 'Discourse discourse: social psychology and postmodernity', in J. Doherty, E. Graham and M. Malek (Eds), *Postmodernism and the Social Sciences*, Macmillan, London.

3   *Journal articles*

We start this section with two book reviews taken from journals, and then go on to show you four other entries for ordinary journal articles.

> Risman, B. (2005), 'Are you cold yet? Have the hot family value wars ended in colder families? Review of *The Commercialisation of Intimate Life: Notes from Home and Work* by Arlie Hochschild', *Contemporary Sociology*, vol. 34, no. 2, pp.128–132.

A book review taken from a journal is entered in exactly the same way as a journal article except for the fact that it contains the title of the book within its title. Though the title of the review is enclosed in inverted commas, the title of the book, *The Commercialisation of Intimate Life: Notes from Home and Work*, is set in italics (or underlined). Here is another example of a reference to a book review published in a journal:

> Hardin, G. (1993a), 'Review of *Fifty Million Californians?* by Leon Bouvier', *The Social Contract*, vol. 3, no. 3, pp. 218–219.

Journals usually come out more than once a year, often in four issues (or 'numbers'), but sometimes in fewer and sometimes in more. 'Volume' refers to the year. 'Volume' is usually abbreviated to vol. and 'number' to no. So Risman's book review came out in the 34th year in which *Contemporary Sociology* had been published and in its second issue, or 'number', in that year.

> Kendall, L. (2000) '"Oh no! I'm a nerd!" Hegemonic masculinity on an online forum', *Gender & Society*, vol. 14, no. 2, pp. 256–274.

Kendall's piece is a straightforward article reporting the author's own research. Note that the final entry for a journal article gives page numbers, starting from the page where the article begins to the page where it ends. You only need to provide page numbers in the list of references for journal articles; books and chapters in edited collections do not need them. The reason is this. Journal editors often number the pages of one year's supply of a journal, or one 'volume', in a consecutive way so that vol. 3, no. 1, begins with page 1, while vol. 3, no. 4, begins with, say, page 229 or page 785. And libraries often bind a collection of journal issues together in order to store them more efficiently. (The bound volume on the shelf may be the equivalent of one 'volume' of the journal or, to save money, the library may bind two or more 'volumes' together.) This can make a 'book' of quite formidable proportions, maybe as long as a thousand pages. When you give the date, the volume number, the issue number, and the page numbers, you make it easier for a reader to locate your source quickly.

> Farquharson, K. (1999), 'Racialised media discourses in the "New" South Africa: the Makgoba controversy', *Research in Politics and Society*, vol. 6, pp.175–194.
>
> Markus, A. (1984), 'Labor and immigration: policy formation', *Labour History*, vol. 46, pp. 21–33.

Markus (1984) and Farquharson (1999) are also journal articles. There are no numbers for the issues because the journals, *Labour History* and *Research in Politics and Society*, only come out once a year. This is unusual. You can make a note in your bibliographic record if you come across a source that does not behave in the expected way. Then, if the person marking your essay doesn't know about this and scribbles 'no.?' beside the entry in your list of references, you can explain the situation.

Here is another journal article, this time one that appeared in the first issue of the first volume of a journal:

> Price, C. (1993), 'Ethnic intermixture in Australia', *People and Place*, vol. 1, no. 1, pp. 6–8.

4   *Government publications*

> *Australian Social Trends* (2002), Australian Bureau of Statistics, Canberra (Catalogue number 4102.0).
>
> ABS (Australian Bureau of Statistics), (2004), *Australian Social Trends*, Canberra (Catalogue number 4102.0).

Australian Social Trends is an example of a government publication published by the Australian Bureau of Statistics (ABS) in Canberra. The ABS produces a vast array of publications, and each has an ABS catalogue number. If you quote this number when you are listing ABS material, it will make the task of locating your source much easier for your readers. Note that we have shown the reference in two different formats. You may use either format in your reference list (though ABS publications are usually referred to by their title). If you used the first format, you would refer to the publication in your text as (*Australian Social Trends*, 2004: 47–49) as we have done in this chapter. If you used the second format, your in-text reference would look like: (ABS, 2004: 47–49).

> PIC (Population Issues Committee), National Population Council (1992), *Population Issues and Australia's Future*, Australian Government Publishing Service, Canberra.

PIC (1992) is another monograph, but this time it's a government publication produced by a committee. If you used initials as an abbreviation in the text, repeat them here. If you used them repeatedly in your in-text references, the entry in the list of references should appear under PIC with the full name of the committee spelled out in brackets afterwards. This is because the reader will be looking for PIC, not the full name.

5 *Legal documents*

The reference for an Act needs to include its short title, jurisdiction, and section number (if you are referring to a specific section). The short title is listed within the Act itself, and consists of the name of the Act and the year it was approved. The jurisdiction is where the Act was passed. In Australia, this is the state or territory (abbreviated as ACT, NSW, Vic, NT, Qld, SA, Tas, WA), or the Commonwealth (abbreviated as Cth). The jurisdiction is included unless it is absolutely clear from the title of the Act what the jurisdiction is. If your reference to an Act is to a particular section or sections you have to include the number(s) of these in your reference. As we explained, Acts are divided into sections, and sections are divided into subsections or paragraphs. Each of these divisions needs to be listed as applicable. Section is abbreviated as 's' or 'ss' for multiple sections. Here is an example:

Tobacco (Amendment) Act 2000 (Vic) s 7.

In this example, the section being referred to is section 7. (See our example 15 in **The references in your text**.)

A reference to Case Law includes the names of the parties in italics separated by a 'v' (for example, *Jones v Smith*) followed by the year (either the year the case was decided or the year it was listed in a law report). If the case is listed in a law report, the names and year are followed by the volume number, the abbreviated title of the report series, the number of the first page, and the pinpoint (also called the citation reference point). Most law report series have standard forms of abbreviation. These are usually located at the front of each volume, and they are usually initials. The pinpoint is the page number in the report that you are referring to. Here is an example:

Commonwealth v Tasmania (1983) 158 CLR 1, 2.

As you can see, in this case the reference list entry is the same as the in-text citation in example 15. Here, the plaintiff is the Commonwealth of Australia and the defendant is Tasmania. The year the case was decided was 1983. The case was reported in *Commonwealth Law Reports*, abbreviated as CLR. The volume it appeared in was 158. The first page of the case was on page one of CLR. The pinpoint, or the page that we are referring to, was page two. If the case has a popular name, you could also include it, but this is optional. The popular name would go in parentheses at the end of the reference. Legal documents may seem a little tricky when you first come across them. How is a general reader meant to know that CLR stands for *Commonwealth Law Reports* and that 158 means volume 158? If you were to spell these details out in an undergraduate social science essay, you'd be unlikely to be reproved.

Fortunately many legal documents are now available online. Take care to download them from reputable sources such as government websites. (See, for example, the Australian Legal Information Institute at <http://www.austlii.edu.au/>.)

Legal documents often have different referencing requirements from other types of documents that you might use. If this section has not answered your questions, we recommend that you consult the *Australian Guide to Legal Citation* (Melbourne University Law Review Association Inc., 1998). The *Australian Guide to Legal Citation* can be downloaded from the Internet free of charge from <http://mulr.law.unimelb.edu.au/aglc.asp>.

6 *Electronic references*

There is not yet an established standard for the formatting of electronic references. However, the principle of providing enough information so that your reader can check your reference still applies.

For electronic documents that are essentially photocopies of existing publications, insert them in your reference list as you would the publication itself. For example, a PDF of a journal article would be entered into your reference list just like any other journal article.

For a journal article that you have downloaded from the Internet (perhaps from an online database) in HTML format, you need to enter most of the details that you would for a regular journal article, and you also need to acknowledge that you accessed the article online and where and when you did so. For example:

> White, R., Trante, B. & Hanson, D. (2004), 'Share ownership in Australia: the emergence of new tensions?' *Journal of Sociology*, vol. 40, no. 2 pp. 99–121 [online via InfoTrac] (accessed 9 May 2005).

In the example above, the article was accessed via an online database called InfoTrac. Because InfoTrac is a subscriber-based service and was accessed through a library website, the web address (or URL) would not be accessible to people other than users of that particular library, so it has not been included. Someone interested in looking up this reference would be able to find it by looking up the *Journal of Sociology*, vol. 40, no. 2. If you are using the HTML version of a published article, you do need to say that you accessed the article online because your page numbers will not match those in the printed version of the journal and will have been put in square brackets in your in-text citation.

Some journals are only available online. A reference from one of these would look like the following:

> Critchley, C., & Turney L. (2004), 'Understanding Australians' perceptions of controversial scientific research', *Australian*

Journal of Emerging Technologies and Society, vol. 2, no. 2 [online], available at <http://www.swin.edu.au/sbs/ajets/ journal/issue3/abstract_understanding.htm> (accessed 11 May 2005).

Here we have included the web address for the article. Anyone interested in looking up the article can enter that address in their browser and download it. It's important to include the date that you accessed the article. This is because websites come and go, and if someone looks it up and it's not there, you can at least claim that it did exist on the date you accessed it.

What about web documents that have nothing to do with journals and journal articles? Here you record the author of the document, the date, the title, and URL.

Swords, T. (n.d.), 'Girl power: raising smart, bold girls', [online] available at <http://preteenagerstoday.com/resources/ articles/girls.htm> (accessed 11 May 2005).

Sometimes, as in the following example, there is no named author.

DEST (Department of Education Science and Training) (n.d.), 'Higher Education', [online] available at <http://www.dest. gov.au/sectors/higher_education/default.htm> (accessed 11 May 2005).

Note that in both references above there were no obvious dates on the web pages so we have included 'n.d.', which stands for no date, in place of the date. This lets your reader know that you have looked for a date and couldn't locate one. The first reference, by Swords, had an author listed. The second reference is to the DEST website. Since DEST is the organisation behind the website, we have listed it as the author.

Some web documents don't have obvious authors or companies/ organisations responsible for them. Those can be recorded under their title.

'Glossary of Jamaican Reggae-Rasta words, expressions, and slang' (n.d.), [online] available at <http://www.speak jamaican.com/glossary.html> (accessed 11 May 2005).

Emails can be listed in a reference list under the name of the sender in the following format:

Ahmed, J. (jahmed@university.edu.au) (8 August 2005), 'Working in cyberspace', personal email to P. Williams (pwilliams@company.com.au).

In the example above, 'working in cyberspace' is the title of Ahmed's email to Williams. This is a made-up reference because you need to get permission before quoting from emails, posts to email discussion lists, and Internet chats, particularly if you are quoting the person's email address. If you don't get such permission, you may be breaking copyright regulations. Plus, it's just polite to ask for permission before using somebody else's words, especially if it was a private letter to you (or someone else).

Posts to email discussion lists and online communities can be listed as follows respectively:

> J.J. (10 January 2005) '[Air-l] Pew Internet report on the future of the Internet' on Air-l [email discussion list], available at <http://listserver.dreamhost.com/pipermail/air-l-aoir.org/2005-January/006947.html>.

> badhairday (21 May 2005) 'Static and jumping on wma files' posted to General Software Stuff [online forum], available at <http://www.bleedingedge.com.au/forum/viewtopic.php?t =1074>.

In the first example J.J. is the name the person has used to make their post, their username. Likewise, in the second example the author, badhairday, is the person's username. We do not know what his or her actual name is, but we do know that the user badhairday is the author so we have listed the reference under that name. The phrases in inverted commas are the titles of the authors' posts.

You might like to refer to something written in a weblog (blog). The format is the same as above, but instead of putting 'email list' or 'online forum' in the square brackets, you put 'weblog'.

Technically, if something is published on a website, it is considered published. However, many participants in email discussion lists are not aware that their posts are archived online for all to see. There are no hard and fast rules about when you can refer to an online personal document without permission, but it's best to err on the side of caution. For more information about this, see the document 'Ethical decision-making and Internet research: recommendations from the aoir ethics working committee' (Ess and AoIR ethics working committee, 2002), available online at <www.aoir.org/reports/ethics.pdf>.

You may now be feeling rather overwhelmed. How will I ever learn all these details? What happens to people who put the comma in the wrong place? Are they failed at once? Is there no court of appeal?

Don't panic. Hold onto the principles and the details will, with a little practice, take care of themselves. Remember the first (and major) reason behind the idea of referencing? You are telling people where the evidence you used came from so that, if they wish, they can check it for themselves. It is this that gives weight to the argument expressed in your essay. It is not simply your personal, perhaps uninformed, point of view; it is a reasoned opinion, grounded in the evidence. But if others are to accept it, they must be able to check that evidence. The method outlined here gives them the information they will need to do this.

The information is essential. You must provide date, publisher and place of publication (or journal, volume, number, and pages, or author, title and URL), but you will find some books and articles that use the author/date system and punctuate it, or set it out, in slightly different ways. Variations in punctuation and setting out are not particularly important but the information is. We recommend that you adopt a consistent style, and the one we have presented here is widely accepted, but the key issue is the inclusion of all relevant information.

If you have not been used to documenting your work, using a system of referencing does take a little practice, but you will be surprised at how soon it becomes automatic (and at how critical you will become of authors who offer unsubstantiated assertions). While you are learning, go back over the examples we have used and check the source you want to enter against them. Is this a monograph? Is it a chapter from an edited collection? Is it a journal article? Is it an ABS publication? Is it some other type of government publication written by a committee? Is it a legal document? Is it a web document or other online source? Decide which category your source falls into and then enter it in the same way as the appropriate example. (You can put the full bibliographic details into your 'References' section at the same time as you make the first in-text citation. If you're using bibliographic software, it does this for you automatically.)

Perhaps in some rare case you will use a source that is not like any of the examples here. This is not the end of the world. Simply remember the *reason* behind the method and make sure that you provide your readers with all the information they will need if they are to locate your source. Take the example of a newspaper article. If the journalist's name is given you could enter it like a journal article but with a much more specific date (day and month as well as year, instead of volume, number and year). If the journalist is not named you could use the name of the newspaper itself. If the source is something like the minutes of the Glenwood Tennis club you could put '(Minutes, 13/9/05)' in your text and, in the list of references, include the address of the secretary so that a reader could write and get a copy. But in cases like this it's a good idea if students append a photocopy of the rare and unusual source. In this case your in-text reference would read '(Minutes, 13/9/05, see Appendix 1)'.

The numbered footnote system

The numbered footnote system is more often used in the humanities than the social sciences. It has some disadvantages when compared to the author/date system but in other respects it is superior. The main disadvantage is that it can mean more work for your reader if they want to keep track of the sources you are using. Footnotes appear at the bottom of each page; if they come at the end of an essay they are technically endnotes. But we'll use the term *footnotes* for both. Word processing software makes placing footnotes and endnotes very easy.

The numbered footnote system has two main advantages. Unlike the in-text citations of the author/date system, the numbers in the text are relatively unobtrusive. If readers are not interested in checking the sources, they can easily ignore the numbers and lose themselves in the flow of the text. Also words that expand the meaning of the text can be added to the footnotes documenting the source of the quote, or statement of fact. In principle it's best to avoid extensive use of footnotes for this purpose but, in practice, some topics, or some approaches to topics, do require it. For example, if you wished to cater both to the general reader and the specialist, more technical material might be relegated to the footnotes. (Whatever you do, make sure that you don't put major findings in your footnotes!)

Never mix the two systems of references. Never document some sources with in-text citations and others with numbered footnotes.

With the numbered footnote system you place a number in your text at the point where you wish to document your material and the reader locates the appropriate reference by this number, either at the bottom of the relevant page or at the end of the essay. We recommend the bottom of the page because it's easier for readers.

A copy of a student's essay using the numbered footnote system is included in Appendix 1. The topic is:

> Analyse the main themes expressed by C. Wright Mills in his book *The Sociological Imagination* and briefly evaluate the contribution it has made to sociology.

Read it through and see how the system works. (Later you can read it critically, not as a specimen illustrating a system of referencing, but as an evaluative argument on a theoretical topic.)

As you can see, with this system the first time a work is referred to, full bibliographic details are given, including page numbers. Here 'p.' indicates 'page' and 'pp.' indicates 'pages'. The letters 'ff.' stand for 'following' and indicate that the pages following the one noted are also relevant. This is a rather vague way of indicating page references but at least it gives the reader a fixed point to start with. (Some forms of punctuating the in-text part of the author/date system use 'p.' and 'pp.' instead of a colon, and 'ff.' may be used in either system.)

In the first reference to a given work full bibliographic details are set out. On subsequent occasions the terms 'ibid.' or 'op. cit.' are used. Ibid. is an abbreviation of the Latin word *ibidem* which means 'in the same place', and op. cit. is an abbreviation of the Latin phrase, *opere citato*, meaning 'in the work cited'. Ibid. is used by itself if a reference is exactly the same as the one that precedes it and with a page number if it is the same reference but a different page (or pages) is being referred to. Op. cit. is used after the author's name on all other occasions when the work has already been cited in full. If you are using more than one source by the same author, subsequent references should also include the date of the particular source you are referring to as well as the surname and the phrase 'op. cit.'

(Occasionally, you will see the term 'loc. cit.', *loco citato*, meaning 'in the place cited'. Just think of it as virtually a synonym for op. cit., which it virtually is.)

There are more variations in the way in which the numbered footnote system is used than is the case with the author/date system. Though most modifications retain the use of ibid. a number have dropped the use of op. cit. and use the author's surname and a short version of the title instead. Again, these details are relatively unimportant. But the principle remains the same; sufficient information must be provided to enable readers to locate the sources referred to.

Because full bibliographic details are given the first time a work is cited it is not, strictly speaking, necessary to provide a list of references at the end of the essay. But hunting back through the footnotes for the occasion when a work was first referred to can be tedious, and if a final list of references is provided, it's easier for people to follow up your sources.

By now you are probably puzzled, firstly about why there should be more than one system of referencing, and secondly about why there should be variations within the two major systems in the way they are set out. This diversity was not established with the deliberate intention of creating arbitrary bureaucratic traps for unsuspecting students as they attempt to satisfy the demands of different departments and different institutions (though we are well aware that it can have this effect).

Students might take consolation from the fact that their teachers face the same problem when they are writing for publication. We are intrigued to find that EndNote and other types of bibliographic software provide literally hundreds of systems of referencing to accord with the requirements of various journals. Some of these systems are based on the author/date system, others on numbered footnotes. If your article is rejected by *Nature*, with a few taps of the keyboard you can change the format of the references into one acceptable to the *Journal of the American Psychological Association*. Users also have the possibility of creating new styles of their own. Students might find it helpful to create 'styles' that meet the precise requirements of different subjects.

We know of no sociological study which explains the diversity in systems of referencing. It probably evolved as part of an unintended chain of consequences as different groups of scholars and publishers tried to standardise practices in different places, with different needs and priorities and without the resources (or the inclination) to arrange a summit conference. Or, maybe, the explanation is simply that when Moses came down from that mountain he had forgotten to ask God about referencing. You can always dodge the worst of the bureaucratic traps if you remember the reason behind the idea of referencing, provide the information your reader needs to locate your source, and aim for a consistent style. If you do this, *no one* is going to mark you down for putting the comma in the 'wrong' place in your first essay.

Plagiarism

Plagiarism is committed when authors fail to acknowledge that words and/or ideas have been borrowed. Specifically, it is committed when:
- verbatim phrases and passages are used without quotation marks and/or without a reference
- an author's work is paraphrased and presented without a reference
- a direct reference is given to authors the student has not read (but has, perhaps, read about)

- other students' essays are copied
- essays are written in conjunction with other students (without prior permission)
- an essay has already been submitted for assessment in another course.

Plagiarism is a serious offence. It is a way of cheating to get higher marks for less effort (or to gain a job, promotion or prestige that the plagiarist has stolen rather than earned). Students who plagiarise can lose their university place and academics who do the same can lose their positions.

It is possible to plagiarise accidentally. This can happen when a student takes notes from an author and later on forgets that these notes were someone else's words and ideas and not their own. This is one of the reasons why we emphasised the importance of distinguishing between your own ideas and those of your source when you are taking notes. (See Chapter 3.) The accidental plagiarist faces a heavy burden of proof.

A few beginners might be termed 'naive plagiarists'. They think that the sources have said it all so much better than they ever could and that it would be presumptuous to try to express their own ideas. So they copy out the words of the great masters as an act of homage. They are misguided and will be fortunate if the examiners conclude that they are merely naive.

Some students discuss essay questions at length with friends, or they ask someone to read a draft of their essays to check their English expression. Is this legitimate? Discussing your work with other students is one of the best ways of learning. But you need to draw a clear line between talking in a group and writing up alone. If you want to get a friend to proofread a draft and check the English for you, ask your tutor if this is acceptable.

Fraud

If a so-called researcher claims to have done some primary research and invents the data this is not plagiarism but fraud. It is a serious offence. Everyone, students and established researchers, should be scrupulously careful when collecting and recording data. They should also keep all working documents produced during the course of their research in case questions arise later.

Activities

1. Choose excerpts from three of your textbooks. Paraphrase them (be sure to write down the references). Does paraphrasing help you to understand the excerpts? What is the difference between your indirect quotes (paraphrases of the excerpts) and the quotes themselves?
2. Write sentences with the following types of in-text references:
   - an indirect quote from a journal article
   - a statement of fact from a book
   - a direct or indirect quote from a chapter in an edited book
   - an indirect quote from an electronic document
   - a direct quote from a website.
3. Compile a reference list for the sources you drew on in activity 2.

Chapter 6
Writing a Research Report

Objectives

➤ To understand differences between research in the natural and social sciences
➤ To understand differences between objectivity and subjectivity in social research
➤ To learn how to structure a research report

Outline

➤ Science and social research
➤ Objectivity
➤ Organising the research report
➤ Reports and essays

If you are studying any of the social sciences, at some time in your undergraduate career you will probably do a course (or courses) on research methods, and may find that this involves doing some practical work and writing a report on it. For a number of students, especially those with a background in humanities, this can seem like a betrayal. No sooner have they mastered the art of essay writing than they are presented with what appears to them to be a request to write something quite different, with seemingly alien and rigid requirements. The arbitrary bureaucratic jungle, with its unfathomable rules, savage punishments and merciless enforcers, is closing in again.

When you come to write up practical work your department will provide you with more help than is feasible to give in this book. Here we cannot assume that you have any specialised knowledge of research procedures, and of the different merits and problems associated with various methods. There is little point in our suggesting ways in which their idiosyncrasies should be tackled in a report. Our aim is not to offer you specific help with specific questions, but rather to talk about research reports in a general way, and to show you the principles on which they are based. When you understand these principles you will understand why certain information must always be presented, and why a research report is usually arranged under a number of conventional headings. Having understood this, you will not need to waste emotional energy worrying about matters of form but will be able to devote yourself to the more rewarding question of content.

We will show you that the idea that research reports are unlike essays (and that their presentation is governed by rigid and irrational rules) is wrong. Research reports are very much like essays and, just as is the case with essays, there are good reasons for the rules governing the way they should be documented and set out.

When you write an essay you are testing your argument against theories and information available in published sources. This is research. If you do it well, you are making a contribution to knowledge. But sometimes the information you need is not already available in books and journals, or it is available but not in a form that meets your needs. If this is the case, and if it is really important to your argument, you may decide to do some extra work to discover what this missing information actually is, and whether it does or does not support your argument. The two processes are described as 'secondary analysis' and 'primary analysis'. When we talk of research using existing material (such as articles from the library) we call this secondary analysis, and when we talk of research where researchers actively generate and collect data in order to meet their particular needs, we call this primary analysis.

Writing a research report is like writing an essay in that, in both cases, you are setting down your ideas and demonstrating to your readers that you have made an honest attempt to check them against the evidence. The feature that can make a research report unlike an essay is that, if it involves primary analysis, your readers do not have direct access to your evidence. They can't look it up in the library and see if it is valid evidence for the point you are making and if you have used it correctly. It is this characteristic of reports based on primary analysis that makes them different from essays. It means that, in the text of your report, you have to do two things. First, you have to convince others that you have indeed put your ideas to a fair and valid test. Second, you must provide full information on how you went about this. By providing this information, you allow them, if they wish, to try as nearly as possible to do exactly what you did and see if they get the same results. You allow them to replicate your primary analysis.

Obviously this is much more trouble than checking your assertions about facts published in books or articles, and you must provide all the information that they will need if they are to do it. This is the principle underlying progress in the natural sciences. Primary research should be repeatable because, if other scientists can repeat an experiment and get the same results, the theory tested by the experiment can be accepted as a contribution to knowledge. In fact, most readers will not want to replicate your work but your description of your methods is not only a recipe for them to follow, it is also an account that allows them to judge how carefully you went about your work.

They can ask themselves two questions: 'Do I really believe this person did the work as claimed?' And, 'Assuming this is so, am I sufficiently impressed by the research methods to accept the results?' Readers often pay writers the courtesy of belief. They accept that we carried out the research in the way we say we did. The description of the techniques then becomes, not so much a formula for them to follow in order to check up on us, but an account that they use to assess the value of our results.

But they don't have to believe us. The detailed record of our research methods gives research based on primary analysis its empirical (or objective) anchor because it allows others to replicate our work. There is, however, a difference between the social and natural sciences which we should mention so as not to leave you with a false impression. This difference lies at the heart of the question of whether the social sciences are sciences in the same way as physics and chemistry are sciences, and whether, if they are not, there is any point in trying to make them be so.

Science and social research

The people who constitute the subject matter of social research think, interpret, remember, communicate, and can use the understandings gained from these processes to change the way they organise their lives. Animals that are the subjects of biological research certainly feel, and may remember. But their powers of reasoning and communicating with each other are limited, at least insofar as these attributes may affect research. The objects of research in the physical sciences do not think, feel, or remember, and so do not bring any subjective qualities of their own to the research process.

This difference in the subject matter of social science can present difficulties for the principle of repeatability. Even if others were to repeat your research exactly, circumstances could have changed and the social world they were examining might, in some respects, be unlike the one you looked at. Of course, this could happen with a natural science. Perhaps the climate has changed and the rare lichen no longer grows at an altitude of 1200 metres? But the particular difference with the social sciences is that the research itself can change the circumstances. This is because the human participants have understood it and used it as a basis to change what they do. Your research itself may have changed the circumstances and, because of this, others will not be able to repeat what you have done and get exactly the same results. (For example, opinion polls can influence politicians to alter their decisions and the policies that flow from these decisions. This in turn may affect public opinion. Next time there is a poll, the results will be different.)

This is not the only reason why the social sciences cannot be exactly the same as the natural sciences. For example, unlike laws of nature, social laws and social conventions are not immutable; they can be, and often are, changed. And people may decide to disobey them and risk the consequences. Nevertheless, the possibility of research itself affecting future social conditions and future human behaviour is a key example of the way in which humans' capacity to reflect and make choices can make social research different from research in the natural sciences.

If you want to be a scientist who can discover social regularities and predict human behaviour as an astronomer predicts eclipses, the tendency of social research to affect social behaviour will be frustrating. But you could see this interaction between the researcher and the researched in a positive and hopeful light. It can mean that human beings are able to achieve a better understanding of their circumstances. Unlike the rare lichen passively dwindling to extinction, they don't have to be overwhelmed by their circumstances. Instead, with the help of the sociological imagination, they may be able to take some steps to control them. Research in the social sciences can be hard to replicate exactly, and this, in turn, may throw doubt on its reliability. Social research, however, is not only involved with the work of describing and explaining the social world, it is also a part of the way in which that world is changed.

Objectivity

How can research that gets involved in the world, intentionally or unintentionally, and that affects that world, be value-free? How can it be objective? Many students think about these questions and come to the conclusion that social research cannot be objective. They may then give up their studies. Or they may decide to become committed activists and let the goal of finding out about how society works take second place to the goal of working for political change. We don't want to discourage anyone from committing themselves to social reform. The world needs it. But it's a pity if people decide too quickly that objective knowledge is impossible, if only because reforms are more effective if they are based on sound knowledge of how the existing situation works.

Is it really impossible to gain some objective knowledge about society? Some of the doubts about this are only based on confusion about words. The terms *objective* and *subjective* have a number of meanings, and people often jump from one meaning to another and then to a conclusion without realising what they are doing. We have put together a table of different meanings for this pair of words (see pages 88 to 89). Perhaps you will be able to add to it.

Don't worry now about the finer details in the objective/subjective table. You will find out more about emics and etics and event causation in the course of time. What we want to show you in the table is that the word *objective* is used in a number of ways. When people say 'You can't be objective' it's important to know what kind of objectivity they feel is beyond their reach. If they are saying that they can't avoid bias #2, we agree. Whether it's a question of social or natural science, bias #2 is inevitable. But it is possible at least to minimise bias #1.

Research methods texts that discuss valid and reliable measures, good sampling techniques and procedures for checking hypotheses, are all talking about ways of cutting down on bias #1. We may not be able to eliminate it, but it is absurd to say we can't try to reduce it. We can also look for empirical evidence, keeping the non-empirical kind for our own private inspiration. If we do choose to use 'subjective measures' we will do it with our eyes open and with a clear goal in mind. We may want to do 'subjective research' on the reasons people have for acting as they do, and the hopes, worries, loves and ambitions that motivate them. But if we do we will try to avoid mistakes and systematic errors, to maximise the use of empirical evidence, and to write about what we have found as clearly as possible. It is possible to investigate people's subjective worlds 'objectively'.

Organising the research report

Let's now put questions about the interaction between research and human behaviour and of the nature of social science to one side for

OBJECTIVE	SUBJECTIVE
unbiased	**biased with bias #1** Bias #1 can range from honest mistakes and muddles, to systematic errors which result in researchers finding want they want to find, to outright fraud. We can and should try hard to avoid this kind of bias. (Many of the techniques you learn in a research methods course help you to minimise bias #1.)
	biased with bias #2 Bias #2 involves selecting a topic. We cannot research everything and we tend to chose topics that interest us, and our interests are formed by our values. Even if we choose boring topics we are still neglecting all the other potential areas of research. We cannot avoid the 'bias' of choosing a topic.
empirical evidence Empirical evidence is evidence that other people, apart from the researcher, can see (or hear, touch, taste or smell). This is the 'objectively available evidence' discussed in Chapters 4 and 5. For example, if you say that there are six lanes in a swimming pool this may not be true but it is an empirical (or objective) statement. Other people can check the pool and count the lanes to see if the statement is accurate or not.	**non-empirical 'evidence'** If evidence is only available to the researcher it is not empirical. For example, a researcher's feelings or emotions or dreams cannot be played on a TV screen for other people to look at. If someone says 'I feel happy' or 'I dreamt last night about flying' we just have to decide whether we are going to accept this or not. There is no empirical way of checking the correctness of such statements.
an objective measure This is a system of classification (or 'measuring instrument') that can be applied to more than one case (or person) and which can be used by other researchers besides the one who devised it. For example,	**a subjective measure** This is a system of classification, or measuring instrument, that can only be applied to one case (or person). For the next case (or person) it is different. For example if you ask people 'What social class do you

a researcher could draw up a list of occupations and divide them into upper, middle and lower class occupations. Others could then ask people their occupations and use the list to classify these people according to their 'social class'. This may not be the best way to measure social class but it is 'objective'. Anybody could use the list and end up classifying respondents in the same way as the original researcher. A project that relied heavily on objective measures might be called a *quantitative* study because it would produce results that would be easy to count and to present in a numerical format.

consider you belong to?' you will get a range of answers: 'working', 'oppressed', 'ruling', 'superior', 'year 12' and so on. Each person will have their own mental system of classification and their own way of deciding where people fit within it. We can't know if the person claiming to be 'working' class is really worse off than the people who say they are 'ruling class' or 'superior'. There can be good reasons for using 'subjective' self-identification questions (or 'subjective measures') but they do not produce an 'objective' system of classification. A project that relied heavily on subjective measures might be called a *qualitative* study.

unintended consequences

All of our actions and failures to act have many consequences. We are aware of the some of these consequences and actively try to achieve them. Others just happen. For example, when we speak we are trying to communicate with someone else, but one unintended consequence of our action is that we help keep the English language alive. When we shop or pay the rent we are trying to make ends meet until payday, but an unintended consequence is that we help keep the economy going. Researchers who concentrate on studying patterns in unintended consequences may say they are doing 'objective' research. (Or they may say they are studying the latent functions of people's behaviour, or 'event causation', or that they are taking an 'etic', extrinsic or 'outsider's' approach. If a person who has suffered some personal disaster, like losing a job or failing to get a university place, says 'I'm going to look at this objectively and concentrate on the broader context of the problem' we can call this an 'etic' or extrinsic or, indeed, an 'objective' approach.)

intended consequences

Researchers who concentrate on the meaning people give to their actions, the reasons that they have for doing what they do, may say that are doing 'subjective' research. (Or they may say they are studying manifest functions, or agency, or that they are taking an 'emic' or intrinsic approach.)

the moment. Let's talk, not of the central problems in social theory and their relevance to research procedures, but of the immediate topic of this chapter. This is the rationale behind the way in which a research report based on primary analysis is written.

To sum up what we have said earlier; as well as providing a convincing account of the argument you want to develop, the report must do two things:

- It must convince your readers that your primary analysis was done honestly and well.
- It must provide them with the information they will need if they decide that they want to try to replicate the work.

It may be true that most of your readers will not want to replicate your research. But they will certainly want to examine critically the steps you took when you were doing it, so that they can decide whether they should or should not accept your argument. If they do decide to replicate your study, they may not get exactly the same results but, if your work was done well, there will usually be sufficient similarities for them to be convinced that you did do the job properly, and for you both to use the differences as a basis for further research if you wish.

Let's imagine you are writing a report on a research project designed to test a specific hypothesis. A hypothesis is a tentative theory about how something is. This type of research involves analysing evidence to see whether the hypothesis is likely to be correct.

All research does not conform to this pattern. Sometimes your ideas about aspects of society that concern you will not be particularly clear and you will spend time refining a number of research questions, and actually doing research in order to look for a hypothesis or hypotheses that can be tested. Just as you may approach an essay without any clear argument of your own, and as you read and reflect work towards generating one, so may you begin a research project in this way. Or you may be mid-way between these two points and can express the objectives of your research in a clear research question, a sentence that has a question mark at the end. But for simplicity's sake we will assume that you have already found your hypothesis and that you have designed and carried out a research project in order to test it. Your hypothesis and your findings about it will be your argument.

There are as many ways of doing primary research as there are researchers with problems to investigate and the ingenuity to devise valid and repeatable tests of their ideas. Have a look at a book like Neuman (2003), *Social Research Methods: Qualitative and Quantitative Approaches*, or Kellehear (1993), *The Unobtrusive Researcher*, to get some idea of the range of methods that can be employed. The stereotypical social survey is far from being the only weapon in the social scientist's armoury. But this is not a primer on research techniques and we will use the example of a social survey because it is probably one that will seem familiar to you. Though the way you write up a project will vary according to the methods that you have used, if you organise your work under the headings used in the example below you are not likely to leave anything out.

So how are you going to organise your report on the survey you have just completed? We're going to use the example of writing a research report on the topic of 'attitudes on campus to attempts at religious conversion' to describe how you could lay out your report.

Attitudes on campus to attempts at religious conversion

Introduction

This introductory section will probably begin with the broader practical and theoretical concerns that led you to this topic, and end with a clear statement of your specific hypothesis (or hypotheses). It will also explain how it was that you got from these theoretical concerns to that hypothesis. This explanation will involve saying why you decided to do research on attitudes to attempts at religious conversion on campus, and why you developed the idea that a person's pre-existing belief system might be a crucial factor affecting attitudes to these attempts.

What did you find in the literature that was relevant to your concerns? Show how it helped you to order your ideas, and document your sources in just the same way as you would with an essay. (You may need a separate sub-heading here: **Survey of the literature**.)

Clarify what you mean by belief system and explain why you decided to divide that concept into three categories: agnosticism; a personalised belief in God; and a belief in God combined with participation in an organised church or sect. How did you define 'conversion attempt'? And what counted as a 'religion': churches, sects, cults, the campus snowboarding club? Explain.

End the introductory section with a statement of your hypothesis.

Hypothesis:

> Attitudes to attempts to convert students to new religions at South Eastern University will be associated with a student's pre-existing belief system. Agnostics and people with a personalised belief system will be more hostile to such attempts than people who both believe in God and belong to an organised church or sect.

The key to successful report writing lies in clearly stating your hypothesis (or hypotheses, or research question) towards the beginning, and making sure that the rest of the report relates back to it. The hypothesis is the essence of your argument, or that aspect of it that you are investigating. The evidence has been gathered as a test to see if the hypothesis can or cannot be left to stand as a statement about the social world. You should also define the key concepts used in the hypothesis: conversion attempt; attitudes towards conversion attempt; belief system; agnostics; people with a personalised belief in God; people who belong to an organised church or sect.

Methods

Discuss here why you thought it a good idea to do a survey and ask questions in order to test this hypothesis. (Implicit in this is that it was the best method to employ, better than, say, standing about and watching, pretending to be a cult missionary yourself, joining a sect to see what the other members were like, checking to see who used the religious centre at lunch time, infiltrating the humanist society, or any one of the many methods you could have used to investigate religious life on campus.)

Why did you think pre-structured face-to-face interviews were better for this topic than other forms of survey research? How did you decide on the questions to ask? Describe the steps you took to make sure they were valid and reliable questions. How well do the questions you asked reflect the key concepts?

You will have done a pilot study, a small trial run of your project. Write about it. Explain how it was that you found out that many people in that study did not understand some of the questions. For example, a number did not know what you meant by 'pantheism', or 'nihilism', or 'animistic belief systems', and you decided that, if you were to get reliable data, you had to change the wording of questions that used these expressions.

Were there problems with the interviewing? Did some people refuse to talk to you? Did some find the questions too personal and did they, perhaps, hide their feelings? Do you think that people's answers varied according to their perceptions of your own religious beliefs? Did anyone mistake you for a missionary who was adopting a particularly subtle approach? Did some people talk about joggers and vegetarians and rather miss the point about religion?

Describe how you selected your sample, and the degree to which you think it represents all students at South Eastern University. (The methods books talk about external validity or the degree to which you can generalise from the people you interviewed to the people you did not interview.)

What ethical problems did this study raise? Describe the steps you took to minimise the chance of causing distress or other problems for the people you interviewed. If necessary you can also discuss the degree to which this may have affected your results.

In this section, you are trying to tell your reader exactly what you did, including the problems you encountered and the mistakes you made, and why you approached the topic in the way you did.

Results

Write out what you discovered. With this project, tables would be appropriate. (See Chapter 8 for details on how to set out tables.) With other projects, where more qualitative data were gathered, your results section would be more descriptive, using words rather than words and numbers. For example, you may have designed a project based on participant observation. What happened to you after you joined the sect of new, reformed, true believers? What were you able to discover about the motivations of your fellow members? If you use tables to report your results, be sure to explain them in your text. Don't leave tables (or graphs) to speak for themselves. They can't. Use them to illustrate what you are saying.

Discussion

Given these results, what has happened to the hypothesis? Is there an association between pre-existing belief systems and attitudes to conversion attempts and, if there is, does it take the form predicted in your hypothesis? Can you take these results at face value? Perhaps some other factor might explain the association. If you have information on this other factor set it out in your results section.

Discuss the extent to which the problems described in your methods section may have undermined your confidence in the patterns set out in your results section. And talk about the possibilities suggested by information you discovered that were not directly related to your hypothesis, but which emerged unexpectedly. Maybe age or gender or ethnic origin made an unforeseen difference to people's attitudes, and this could suggest new hypotheses to you.

Conclusion

Taking all the above into account, can you say that the hypothesis was most likely confirmed, or that it was not confirmed? Given this, set out the implications for the theoretical position you outlined in your introduction. What has happened to your argument now that it has gone through this particular fire?

Appendices

Attach a copy of your survey questions, tables of raw data used to support any other tables used in your text, sampling details, and any further information that would be necessary for someone wanting to replicate your research.

Appendices supplement your text. Don't, for example, put key results in the appendices. A reader should not be forced to look at an appendix in order to follow your argument. Appendices are there for the extra details that keen critics need, as well as people who may want to repeat the project.

You don't have to attach all of the completed interview schedules or other research materials that were produced during the project, but keep everything until your report has been assessed and returned to you. You might need the research materials to show more precisely how you went about the work.

Reports and essays

You see, as we told you, writing a report is like writing an essay. You are concerned with an argument, and with the evidence that this argument is tested against. The exercise of organising the report under conventional headings is not a ritual designed to placate the angry guardians of a scientific cult. It is a convenient way of ensuring that you do not leave anything crucial out. If you think you can get the essential information across without using the conventional format, do so. The format makes the work easier for you, but there is no absolute reason why you must abide by it. (If you are thinking of a particularly innovative layout though, do check the requirements of your department.)

Many books on research methods have a section on report writing. When you reach this stage in your course, read the relevant section in your own textbook, or course outline, carefully. You could also have a look at Neuman (2003), or Esterberg (2002), or Bouma (2004). For an author who is strongly committed to the positive aspects of the interaction between the researcher and researched and who sees this as integral to the practice of sociology, read Wadsworth's chapter 'Saying what you found out' (1997).

We have included a sample research report written by a student in Appendix 2. This research report is for a qualitative project rather than a quantitative one. You might find it helpful to look at this report, and compare it with the one discussed above.

Remember, primary analysis is not the only way of doing research in the social sciences, nor is it always the best way. There is a wealth of information already gathered, stored in libraries, and readily available to you. Maybe you can test your argument quite adequately through the process of secondary analysis, as indeed you do every time you write an essay.

Activities

1. Go to the library's online databases and find a journal article that is a research report. Look at its different sections. Do they have subheadings? Which of the sections that we discussed in this chapter are included?

2. The student's research report in Appendix 2 is structured differently from the project on campus attitudes towards attempts at religious conversion. Does the student's report include all the parts that are in the proposed structure for the project on students' attitudes to conversion attempts? Does the ordering of the sections have an impact on the effectiveness of the report's argument?

3. This activity assumes that you have a research project in one of your current classes. Write an outline of your research report for this class. Be sure to include an introduction, an argument, a clear statement of the research objectives (research question or hypothesis), key concepts, a methods section, a results section and a discussion section.

Chapter 7

Words

Finding an appropriate level

One of the problems students worry about when they are starting to write is this: 'What tone of voice should I use? Should I use the longest words I can find? Should I try to copy the style of some of the books I have read? It was difficult to follow but perhaps that's how you're meant to write here.'

Most of us hate making social blunders in unfamiliar situations but, instead of looking sideways at the nice gentleman in the business suit to see which fork he uses, think about the purpose of what you are doing. You are trying to tell other people about your ideas as clearly and as simply as possible so that they can understand them, evaluate them, and decide whether they agree with you or not. Contributions to knowledge are not made by people who simply rattle the cutlery and, even if they have got something to say, the noise makes it hard to hear.

We know that the social sciences can be full of the most abominable prose, but you are not going to make it worse. You are going to be a communicator. You are going to find things out and will want to tell other people about them in ways that they can understand.

So, our counsel to you is this:

• Never use a long word where a short one will do.
• Keep your sentences short.

- Avoid page-length paragraphs.
- Be careful with pronouns. If in doubt, replace them with a noun.
- Prefer the active voice to the passive voice.
- Try to give concrete examples for abstract words and expressions.
- Use the first person: say 'I think ...' when that is what you mean.
- When you have a draft finished go though it and eliminate all unnecessary words.

Writing simply and clearly is often more trouble than being obscure and long-winded. Even after you have a written draft of your essay which sets out the argument well, you will probably have to go back and rewrite sections to make them clearer and more readable. Computers are invaluable here. You can rewrite sentences and rearrange words with no trouble. But you can't get an overview of the whole paper by reading it in screen-sized sections. For this you need a draft print-out. And a printed draft is much easier for you to edit and evaluate than a hand-written one.

Should you make any concessions to 'academic respectability' when you are choosing your words? Academic writing is more formal than everyday language. We recommend that you avoid slang and abbreviations such as 'etc.', 'e.g.' and 'i.e.' And be careful about contractions like 'can't', 'he's', she's, 'they're', 'won't', 'weren't' and so forth, unless, of course, they are part of direct speech that you are quoting. This is a case of, 'Do as we say not as we do.' We have used contractions in this book because a conversational style is more appropriate for teaching than the more formal style of scholarly articles, books and students' essays. The sample pieces of text in Chapter 3 and the sample papers in the appendices are a better model for you to follow than our example here.

When you are writing about numbers spell out the numerals one to nine in full. (Dates, such as 5 November 2005, and numbers that are part of series, as in Volume 1, or Chapter 6, are exceptions.) Any numeral that starts a sentence should also be spelt out. This can lead to a certain rearrangement of words if you had intended to begin a sentence with the number 462 897.

Sometimes you have to use abstract words and technical expressions because they are more accurate and there is no other way of saying what you want to say. But when you use a phrase like 'relative deprivation' or 'demographic transition', explain what it means. See the sample sections of essays in Chapter 5, examples 4 and 16. The authors have done this for the terms 'relativism' and 'trustworthy' with respect to institutions. When you explain an unfamiliar term both you and your tutor will be confident that you know what it means, and you will find it easier to work with the concept the word represents. One sure road to confusion lies in piling up a welter of specialist terminology that you think you understand but in fact have not quite mastered. Check unfamiliar terms in a reference book oriented towards the social sciences. General purpose dictionaries may be helpful, but discipline-based dictionaries such as *The Penguin Dictionary of Sociology* (Abercrombie et al., 2000) and *The Concise Oxford Dictionary of Politics* (McLean & McMillan, 2003) are often more useful. (Most also include biographical entries; these provide quick help with placing scholars in their historical context.)

What about jargon? *Jargon* is the word that outsiders use for other people's specialist terminology. It's a pejorative word. We don't like feeling excluded so we talk of 'incomprehensible jargon' instead of 'technical expressions' or 'specialist terminology'. Outsiders may be feeling ruffled with good reason. Jargon can be a useful shorthand helping insiders to communicate more effectively but it can also be a means of showing off, of excluding the general public and of protecting ideas from fair criticism. 'Look at me,' says the jargon-user. 'I've learnt the secret words of the inner circle. I expect they wouldn't let you join; you're not clever enough to understand the important things we talk about.'

Usually it's not as bad as this; people using specialist terminology in an inappropriate context have simply forgotten that their audience doesn't know the words. But whether they use jargon by accident or on purpose, they are not going to communicate. So no one will adopt the better policies for homeless people, or for children failing at school, or for long-term unemployed women, because no one in positions of authority or the media can understand the research report. So be careful. Jargon is a useful short-hand but not everyone knows the vocabulary. Check that you know the meaning of a specialist term before you use it and be sure that your audience knows it too.

Good writers know who their audiences are. Picture the person reading your essay. Who is it? Probably it's the same old tutor that you've had all semester. Write for him or her but don't write for him or her alone. Imagine that your essay is so good that it's going to be shown all round the staff room, so try to make your tutor just a little fuzzy in your mind. Write for the intelligent reader who knows something about social science but not much about your specific project.

Writer's block

You want to communicate. You respect your readers and are brimming with good intentions. But you just can't think of any way to begin or of anything to say. In fact, the thought of writing down even the smallest thing may terrify you. This looks like writer's block. It needs treatment before it turns into writer's phobia. What can you do about it?

Try writing on a piece of paper, for your eyes only, why, out of all the topics available, you chose this one and not another. (If you would rather devise another question altogether because something else, related to your course, interests you more, discuss it with your tutor.) However awful the range of possible topics seemed, the one you have chosen must have seemed marginally more interesting because you chose it. Why? It doesn't matter what you write at this stage because you can always change it later.

Try writing what you really think of the books and articles you have read, again for your eyes only. Be as rude as you like. Now that you are feeling better, summarise what they say. Can you concentrate their central ideas into one paragraph or less? You can handle anything as small as that. Have a look at C. Wright Mills doing this to Talcott Parsons (1970: 33–42), Popper to Adorno (1972: 267), or Ellis to Derrida and 'deconstruction' (1989: 69–71). Very satisfying.

As you do these things you will find that you have ideas, a few of which may even be relevant to your question. Now write an answer to the question in a hundred words, any old words. Force yourself to do it. Yes, it's terrible. A three-year-old could have done better. But look what has happened. You have made a start, and the dreaded phobia has slunk off to look for someone else. Now you are free to get on with that superior, sophisticated, scintillating argument that was there all the time just waiting for the rough company to leave.

A minor writer's block can often be treated with a tool like a synonym finder or thesaurus. If you are simply stuck for a word, looking up a similar word and browsing through a range of synonyms may be all that's needed to set you free. Word processing packages have a built-in thesaurus. If you're doing your scribbling at the screen you can use this. Computer-based thesauruses are improving all the time but we haven't yet met one to rival the better ones in print. It's still a good idea to keep a conventional thesaurus as a backstop for your electronic one. Most major publishers (such as Oxford, Random House, and Merriam-Webster) sell them.

It may be that you have a problem with writing because you haven't read enough. In this case don't throw your mini-draft away. It will help you decide which extra sources you need to read and will be useful in keeping the reading focused. How much support can you expect from your tutor at this stage? Tutors won't tell you what to write and they usually won't read a complete draft. They can't do this for all their students, so it would be unfair to do it for one. But they can help if you are having difficulties at this early planning stage. Most will look at a one-page outline, give you some feedback on your approach, and suggest further reading if this is necessary. If you think you would work more confidently after some guidance, get your mini-draft into a form that is fit for the eyes of others and take it in for a consultation.

Your tutor is not the only person to consult. Any discussion with patient listeners will help you clarify your thoughts. Talk to your fellow students but go to other people as well. Do you have an eight-year-old niece who wants to know what students do at university? Try telling her about your essay. Will your grandfather listen? Talk about your ideas to as many people as will hear you out and then listen to what they have to say. Your university probably has a study support unit and you should feel comfortable visiting it. While the people there won't be able to advise you about the essay's content, they will be able to tell you if it's clearly argued.

There is one device that will both help keep the phobias away and expand your understanding of society. This is to keep a large file, perhaps apart from your other notes or perhaps interleaved with them. Write down all the ideas and all the questions that come and go when you are reading, when you are in classes, or when you are simply thinking of something else and things connect. (Keep pencil and paper by your bed. Good ideas can appear at 3 a.m.)

Then when you need it you will have a record of your own thoughts to browse through and you will be amazed at how clever and insightful you have been. You will be so busy congratulating yourself and scooping up ideas for your next essay that you will not hear the phobia scratching at the door and it will give up in disgust and go away. Mills, in his sensible advice on how to do sociology, talks about this technique and how useful he found it. Read his appendix, 'On Intellectual Craftsmanship' (1970: 215–248).

One source of writer's block is the belief that you have nothing to say. Brief summaries of the sources, scribbled private answers to the essay question, and your record of your own thoughts and ideas will all help with this problem. But another source can be that you have too much to say and you don't know where to start. Your ideas are like a big fuzzy woollen fleece with everything connected to everything else. (Reality can be like this too.) But you have to grab a section of the fleece and begin spinning it into a sequential thread. Language, especially written language, is linear. An essay begins somewhere, continues for a while, and then comes to a logical end. If we are going to write about it, life has to be forced into a linear form, a form that comes along one word at a time.

Try writing all your thoughts and ideas on a big sheet of paper. Don't worry about the logical order, just get it all down. Don't be critical of the ideas as you write, just get them onto the paper. Only after the torrent is exhausted do you stop and think. Get some coloured pencils or textas and draw circles in the same colour around ideas that seem to have some association with each other. Draw lines between the circles connecting the scattered ideas. Remind yourself of the kind of essay you are planning. Are you explaining an aspect of social reality or offering a critical appraisal of a theory? How can you fit this abundance of material into a linear argument that suits your topic? Cross out the elements that don't fit, and look at the connections you've drawn between the bits and pieces that do fit. You will be able to answer the essay question now that most of the ideas are captured on paper in front of you. This technique is sometimes called 'brainstorming'; the trick is to suspend critical judgement while you get the ideas down. Use your logical, rational and discriminating capacities afterwards.

Sometimes problems develop after you get a fair way into your essay. You make a start, believe you were going well, and then suddenly run out of wind. The spinning slows and the thread breaks. You stop, full of self doubt and uncertainty. A useful emergency technique here is to make a summary of what you have written so far. Is that what you meant to say? More or less? Good. Make it clearer. No? Why not? Perhaps you have moved away from the question and had started writing about something else. You felt unhappy about it but didn't quite know why. Now you do. Unwind the last bit and draw the argument back into its proper form.

It's often helpful to summarise your argument after you've written the first draft in any case. Then you can be sure that you do *have* an argument. That is the first prerequisite. The next step is to make sure that it's a good argument, a logical and coherent answer to the question, well-grounded in the evidence.

What if you've mastered writer's block for one afternoon but you're afraid that it will come back tomorrow? Try stopping a writing session half way through a sentence. Then you will certainly have something to say next time.

We hope you were able to finish a draft of your essay the week before the due date. Then you can put it aside for five or six days and return with a fresh mind before adding the finishing touches. Even if you can't leave it for a few days, at least have a cup of coffee and go for a walk round the block. Many students are more relaxed about their work when they can see that, come what may, they already have something reasonable down on paper. The extra confidence this brings helps them to make the improvements in both argument and style that lift a piece of work from a good pass to a good credit. Besides, in contrast to the anxiety of making a start, they enjoy playing with, and improving, the near-final product. And if you enjoyed writing it, the chances are that your reader will enjoy reading it.

Writing clearly

A clearly written essay has a structure that allows the reader to follow what the author is saying to its logical conclusion. It brings the reader on a journey and by the end he or she will feel as though a point has been made. How does one write such an essay? Remember the advice we provided at the start of this chapter? We will now explain how to put that advice into practice. We will discuss the basic structure of an essay, the basic structure of a paragraph, and how to link paragraphs effectively. Then we will outline some principles of good writing, explaining how they will help. At the end of this section we will discuss the importance of rewriting your drafts.

Structuring your essay

Essays have three essential parts: an introduction, a body, and a conclusion. The introduction is critical – it sets the stage for the rest of the essay. It (briefly) says what your essay will be about. Most important, it outlines both your argument and the structure that the essay will take. It says what you're going to say. 'Oh no,' you say. 'You can't give away the punch line in the first section! It'll ruin the story!' Actually, the opposite is true.

Academic writing is different from writing a novel, where the climax is often unexpected and the better for it. In academic writing you're trying to convince an audience that your argument is correct. In order to do that, you need to state what your argument is early on so that your audience can tell whether the evidence you are providing is convincing. If you don't set out your argument until the end of your essay, your reader will have to go back and reread it to judge its effectiveness. This is a lot to ask.

The body of the essay is where you elaborate on your argument, providing evidence (in the form of quotes, facts, and so on, supported by your in-text references). The evidence shows that your argument is plausible. Here you will also deal with evidence that undermines your argument and explain why you have rejected it. This will be the longest section of your essay and you may divide it into different subsections.

Your conclusion briefly summarises all the evidence and reiterates your argument. In your conclusion you say what you argued in the previous sections again, highlighting why your argument is best.

As chapter 4 explains, an argument is your informed opinion. If you can manage to develop one, state it clearly at the beginning, provide evidence for it in the middle, and restate it at the end, you'll be well on your way to becoming a successful essay writer.

Structuring your paragraphs

Essays are made up of paragraphs, and paragraphs have their own structure. Each paragraph is like a mini essay: it should have a topic sentence, an elaboration of the topic, and a concluding sentence. The topic sentence says what the paragraph is about. The concluding sentence summarises the paragraph and links it with the next paragraph. Here is an example:

> In the case of cricket, a colonial sport has become a postcolonial one. Indeed, for postcolonial nations, such as India, success on the world stage is a way for them to show their independence (Mills & Dimeo, 2003: 113). Colonies and former colonies view postcolonial sport as a site of resistance (Bale & Cronin, 2003: 5). Winning against the former coloniser is the best sort of win.

The topic sentence of this example paragraph tells us that the paragraph will be about the shift of cricket from being a colonial sport to being a postcolonial one. The middle of the paragraph provides evidence that the shift has taken place. The paragraph concludes by reasserting that cricket is a postcolonial sport now. We would expect that the following paragraph would also have something to do with cricket as a postcolonial sport.

There will be places in your essay where you have to switch from one topic to another. To do this you need a linking sentence, providing a smooth shift from one topic to another. If you have clearly outlined the structure of the essay in your introduction with phrases such as, 'First I will...., next I...., and I conclude by ....' it will be simple for you to switch topics. You can say: 'I now turn to [whatever you said you'd do next in the introduction].' Doing this has the added advantage of telling the reader where he or she is in your essay.

In journalism we often see paragraphs of one or two sentences. Given the structure described above, it should be clear that paragraphs in academic essays usually need at least three sentences: one to introduce the topic of the paragraph, one or more to provide evidence, and one to conclude the paragraph and introduce the following one. In writing your sentences, opt for shorter rather than longer. The longer the sentence is, the more difficult it is to understand. The following example turns one long sentence into four shorter ones.

[The authors begin by arguing that private companies can impose negative externalities, such as pollution, on society.]

Given the free market rules of the emerging global economy and the limitations that concern for national competitiveness is placing on the power of individual governments to impose regulation on their internal, let alone international, markets, we need to understand much better the actual and potential, positive and negative influence companies have on society and what motivates them to manage these 'externalities' in the widest possible social interest. (68 words)

(C. Marsden & J. Andriof, 'Towards an understanding of corporate citizenship and how to influence it', *Citizenship Studies*, vol. 2, no. 2, 1998, p.330)

Here is the revised version:

The free market rules of the emerging global economy limit governments' power to regulate national and international markets. Governments' own concern to maintain national competitiveness adds to these limits. But what are the positive and negative influences companies have on society, actual and potential? We need to know and we also need to understand much better what motivates them to manage these 'externalities' in the widest possible social interest. (69 words, four sentences)

A sentence is a complete thought. Readers must be able to hold it in their short-term memory while they work out what it means. If it's 68 words long it's too big for the short-term memory to cope.

Some principles of good writing

We have included a glossary of grammatical terms in Appendix 3. It explains the different parts of speech and how they should be used. In the following sections, words that appear in the glossary are in **bold**.

We recommend that you use the first **person** in your writing, particularly in your early drafts. Using phrases like 'I will show' or

'I argue' helps clarify your argument. Some departments prefer their students to write in the third **person**. If yours is one of them, once the essay is written you can take out all of the 'I' statements, confident that your argument is clear.

You should try to use the active **voice** as much as possible. Using the first person helps you to do this. You should also provide concrete examples for all abstract concepts. If you give an example it will be clear to your reader that you understand the abstract concept you are using. Here are some examples of the passive and active voice:

Passive: The slave was freed.

Active: Caesar freed the slave.

Passive: The law was passed.

Active: The Howard Government passed the law.

Although you may find it difficult at first, using the active voice as much as you can will greatly improve your writing. This is because the active voice shows who is doing what, while the passive voice obscures it.

Here is an example where the author provides a tangible example of a relatively abstract concept: global markets' capacity to limit national power.

> The rules of the global market limit national governments' power [abstract statement]. For example, the World Trade Organisation may say that, if a government insists that imported tuna be caught in a dolphin-friendly fashion, this is nothing but a restraint on free trade [tangible example].

Students often wonder if they should use the past or present tense for their essay. There is no set rule. We suggest that if you are discussing previous research the past tense is probably more appropriate (since the research did take place in the past). Whatever you decide, try to be consistent throughout.

The importance of rewriting

Good writing means rewriting. Almost no writers are able to write an excellent essay or article in their first draft. Your first draft is where you put down the bare bones of your argument and evidence. It's the frame of the building that will become your essay. Only once the frame is erected will it be possible for you to fill in the walls and add the finishing touches.

Once you have written a draft, read it over carefully. We know this can be an excruciating experience! But it really is important. In reading your draft you should be as critical as possible. Ask yourself: Does this make sense? What is the argument? What evidence have I given to support my argument? Does my conclusion tie things together? Overall, does this make sense and is it convincing?

Think about the body of your essay. Do the paragraphs flow smoothly from each to the next? Should some of them be switched around? How might the flow be improved to make the paper read like a logical progression from introduction to conclusion? After you have critically reviewed your essay for its content (and rewritten it), you should go through and remove unnecessary words. This will make the writing clearer and easier to read. The following passage is the long-sentence example above revised further:

> The global market limits a government's power to regulate the economy, as does the government's own desire to maintain national competitiveness. But what external effects do companies produce, and what might motivate them to manage these effects for the common good?

(41 words, two sentences)

Needless words don't help you explain your meaning; they just get in the way. They take up short-term memory space without adding anything helpful. Your reader will understand you with less effort if you take them out.

The final task in rewriting your essay is to proofread. Do not skip this task! Proofreading means reading over your final draft looking for spelling errors, grammatical errors, and problems with layout. The spell-checkers that come with computer word-processing programs are useful, but they aren't perfect. And sometimes the word is wrong, but it is spelled correctly, like 'net' instead of 'ten'. Most essays will have some small errors, and proofreading is the only way to pick these up.

Grammar and spelling

Most guides to essay writing ask you to use conventional English spelling and grammar. So does this one. Making mistakes may simply detract from your credibility as a scholar (see Goffman, 1971, on the art of impression management) or, more seriously, introduce confusion into your writing. For example, 'affect' and 'effect' have different meanings and students who use them interchangeably create unnecessary misunderstandings.

If the word in the text is correctly spelt but doesn't mean what the author thinks it means (as with 'lay' and 'lie') the mistake remains. In Appendix 5 we provide a list of pairs of words that students often confuse, together with examples of how they should best be used. Grammar books and works on style have longer lists. But in our experience, the words that we have set out in Appendix 5 cause the most trouble.

Once you suspect a mistake, you can check spelling and word-use in a dictionary. Grammar is a little harder. But if you keep your sentences short, you will be less likely to make mistakes. Read your work aloud. Ask yourself if it sounds right. If your tutor makes corrections try to understand what was wrong and why. (You can always ask.)

The most common grammatical mistakes that students make are these:

- Confusions with apostrophes, especially 'its' and 'it's'.
- Failing to provide a sentence with a main **clause** and a **finite** verb.
- Lack of agreement between **subject** and **verb.**
- Confusion with **pronouns.** (The author of the essay knows the **noun** or the noun phrase that the pronoun refers to but the reader doesn't.)
- Sentences which are too long. (Readers have to go back over them several times to get the sense, and long sentences can also hide grammatical mistakes more easily than short ones.)

Apostrophes

In English we use apostrophes to show possession (the boy's dog) and to show that something has been left out in contractions (he's late; they're happy; we can't come).

Sometimes using apostrophes to show possession causes problems because students aren't sure what to do if the noun naming the possessor is plural. If the plural is formed with 's' the apostrophe goes after the 's'. So, if two boys owned the dog, we would write 'the boys' dog'. But if the plural is not formed with 's' (as with men, women, children and people), the apostrophe goes before the 's' and we write 'the children's dog'.

Don't use an apostrophe to show possession with possessive pronouns. Here we have *my, your, his, her, our, their, whose* and *its*. 'Its' is the possessive pronoun that causes the most grief. People confuse it with 'it's', the contraction of 'it is'. Don't. If in doubt, write out 100 times: 'It's a pity, but the dog lost its collar'.

Finite and non-finite verbs

A **finite verb** is a form of a verb that can stand by itself in a sentence. 'James is a boy.' This is a complete sentence with a finite verb (*is*). 'James being a boy.' This is not a complete sentence because it does not have a finite verb and so cannot be used on its own. 'Being' is the present **participle** of the verb *to be*. It is used in forming the **present continuous tense**. We can say 'James is good'. This uses the simple present tense. If we say 'James is being good' we are using the present continuous and the verb *is being* is made up of *is*, which is now functioning as an **auxiliary**, and the present participle, *being*. (The present participle is also used to form the past tense called the **past continuous**, as in: 'James was being good'.) The present participle by itself is not, and never can be, a finite verb. If we don't have a finite verb we don't have a sentence and if we don't have a sentence we're not getting anywhere.

There are present participles, past participles and **infinitives**; all of them are non-finite forms of verbs. Present participles cause the most trouble. Past participles (like the word *eaten* in, 'I have eaten six Mars Bars') seem to know their place. They don't often try to carry off a pseudo sentence on their own. But sometimes students use the infinitive by itself and that doesn't work either. The infinitive is the form of the verb that begins with 'to' as in 'to draw'. We can say 'Judith draws well' or 'Judith likes to draw', but we can't say 'Judith to draw' and leave it at that. Of course this looks obvious in a short sentence. Make it long enough though, and you may forget that you forgot the finite verb.

First, make sure you have a finite verb and then check that it is in a main clause. Some words like *while* and *although* only introduce **subordinate clauses**. If you say: 'While I really like ice cream…' or 'Although he is only six years old…' the reader is hanging about waiting for you to say something else. You do have a finite verb ('am' and 'is') but you don't have a main clause. 'While I really like ice cream, I try not to eat too much of it.' 'Although he is only six, he can sing in tune.' In the first sentence 'I try not to eat too much of it' is the main clause and in the second it's 'he can sing in tune.' The clue to identifying a main clause is to ask if it could stand by itself and be a sentence. These two can.

Much advertising copy is written without finite verbs: 'A life-style for today's world.'; 'Living and sharing together.'; 'With one in three at risk.' These truncated examples of non-sentences make it harder for students to absorb a feeling for the real thing. Good authors occasionally slip in a short 'sentence' without any verb; they do it for dramatic effect. The copywriters are copying them and it's better if we don't copy the copywriters.

Subjects and verbs

The verb *to be* is the only English verb which changes its form with different subjects (I am, you are, she is, we are, they are) but all verbs in the simple present tense add an 's' in the third person singular. *They walk to school every day, but he runs. We watch television but she reads.* You know this rule. But in a long sentence it's possible to forget what your subject is and either to put the 's' form in when you should not or to leave it out when you should put it in. Sometimes quite simple sentences can throw a student off course.

> Fincher argues that research into the effects of heredity and the home environment on child development *remains* inconclusive. (Or is it *remain* inconclusive?)

The subject is 'research' which is singular, so the research remains inconclusive. The problem can be that a student looks back and sees 'heredity and the home environment', thinks these are the subject, and so gives the plural form of the verb (*remain*).

Confusing pronouns

Look at the following sentence.

> Malthus was opposed to welfare benefits for the poor because he felt that they would serve to accentuate their misery.

Will 'the poor' accentuate their own misery or are 'welfare benefits' the culprit? Don't let **pronouns** create ambiguity. Better to spell the meaning out by providing nouns even at the risk of sounding a bit wooden.

> Malthus was opposed to welfare benefits for the poor because he felt that such benefits would serve to accentuate the misery of the lower classes.

If you have trouble with grammar you may find one of the following books helpful: Strunk, White and Angell (2000) *The Elements of Style*; or Strumf and Douglas (2004), *The Grammar Bible*. Strunk, White and Angell is brief and authoritative. But if you know very little formal grammar, for example if you haven't been taught the grammatical terms for the parts of speech, you could find it too condensed. If this is the case try Strumf and Douglas. Lynne Truss's book, *Eats, Shoots and Leaves* (2003), is also useful and good bedside reading as well. Professionals rely on Snooks & Co.'s *Style Manual for Authors, Editors and Printers* (2002).

Have a look to see what's available in your library. If it works on the Dewey system of classification, books on English expression and essay writing will be at call number 808. Most computer programs include grammar checkers. These may pick up some grammatical errors but sometimes the advice they provide is wrong. Try not to rely on these to correct your grammar.

Language biases

We all use language and, most of the time, so long as it does what we want it to, it seems to be simply there, like the air we breathe. But it's not like the air at all; it's a human construction. In fact it's a good example of a social structure. People made it, and are continuing to make it, but not everyone has an equal say about what goes into it and not everyone is equally affected by its rules and its vocabulary.

We were very conscious of this when we were writing: 'Ask yourself if it "sounds right".' This advice will work well if you come from an educated, middle-class, English-speaking background. It may be cruelly inadequate if your background is working class and/or non-English speaking. Do ask your tutor for help if you need it. A tutor may not be able to provide it personally, but there may be special catch-up courses available on campus.

'Correct grammar' (like 'correct accents') comes easily to people who already have advantages and harder to those who do not. As 'conventional' or 'correct' English is the language of power and influence, those who can use it are likely to be people who already have advantages, while those who cannot are likely to be disadvantaged in other respects as well. Language structures reflect power relations and help recreate them for the future. Unfair though it is, it is in the interests of students who have difficulties with conventional English to make the extra effort to learn this code, rather than to continue to use an unconventional code. (Then they can at least choose which code they will use instead of being locked into one that may disadvantage them.)

But there is another way in which language not only reinforces inequality but can also confuse our thinking. Here it may be possible to change the code, and do something about the inequalities it represents. Let us tell you a story taken from an article by Douglas Hofstadter in *Scientific American*.

> A father and his son were driving to the football when their car stalled on a railway line and was hit by an onrushing train. An ambulance sped to the scene but the father was dead. The boy was still alive but in a critical condition. He was taken to hospital and wheeled straight into an emergency operating theatre. A surgeon came in expecting a routine case but on seeing the child blanched and muttered, 'I can't operate on this boy – he's my son.'
>
> (Adapted from Hofstadter, 1982: 14)

This is a grim story, but it is also something of a riddle. How can the boy be the surgeon's child? We will leave it to you to work it out.

Hofstadter tells the story to illustrate the point we want to make. Our traditional use of language is often based on the assumption that important people, people with power and status, perhaps the only people who count at all, must be men. As long as we keep on saying 'man' when we mean 'people' and 'he' when we mean 'he or she' we are doing our bit to keep this assumption going.

We do not necessarily change assumptions like these by altering our use of language but, by refusing to exclude women in our writing about human society, we can begin to modify them. More accurate and more inclusive language practices are still being developed. We cannot and would not wish to provide you with a list of rules. Rather, we want to remind you of a deeply taken-for-granted mode of speaking, writing and thinking so that you can make a contribution to forging a different mode, as fluent, as elegant, and as clear as any other, but far more faithful to the reality of people's lives. You can experiment by avoiding gender-specific terms or by making sentences into the plural using 'they' instead of 'he' (as in 'Workers find that they ...' instead of 'The worker finds that he ...'), or you can use 'he or she' instead of just 'he'. A good test is to ask: 'Could a woman reading this imagine that it might refer to her and her concerns as readily as a man, or has my way of writing excluded her from the start?'

If we want to communicate with as wide a range of readers as possible it makes sense not to offend and exclude whole categories of people. But the idea that we change inequalities by monitoring our speech is probably exaggerated. Clear thinking and clear writing depend on clear concepts. It is more important that you as an author know what you are saying than it is to take care not to offend any special interest group by your choice of words. Too much anxiety about the ideological effects of choosing one word instead of another could even inhibit a writer's capacity to analyse social problems and prevent them from finding a way to ameliorate them.

Hofstadter told the story about the surgeon to illustrate his claim that we use 'default assumptions' when we think, and that the 'default' human, the person we imagine when we have no further information, is male. When you are using a computer you set your default margins, font, page size and so on. Then you forget about them and get on with the real business of writing. We can't manage without default thinking because we need to take some things for granted in order to get on with finding out how the world works. But it is always possible that some of our 'default assumptions' are unhelpful. Rather than allowing us to reach useful conclusions efficiently, they may hide important aspects of the world from us. It's a good exercise to take them out and look at them from time to time to time. (How old was your surgeon? Did he have a specific ethnic background?) Does your default human being help you see the world more clearly or should you change the margins and move to a new font?

It's one thing to avoid writing 'Man, from the beginning of history, has been an inventor and discoverer'; it's something else to make a fetish of politically correct language. We try to write in an inclusive way because this helps us to think more clearly, but the objective is communication. Describing and explaining the world is more important than finding a new way of saying 'manhole' or 'ombudsman'.

Obscurity

There is another kind of language bias that we should also watch out for and avoid – wilful obscurity. Some writers are hard to understand because the subject that they are writing about is unfamiliar and we, as readers, don't have the background to understand them. They are specialists writing for specialists and we are locked out of the communication. If we want to join in, we have to do some homework. A reader should not expect to understand a book on medieval Greek without knowing some Greek, or one on general relativity without mathematics.

But if authors claim to be writing for social scientists, or for the educated general public, we should be able to understand them. In Chapter 3 we talked about difficult texts. Clearly, first-year students will experience problems with texts that third-year students will not, but difficulties are not always due to the student's lack of background.

Sometimes the writer is lazy. Scholars may have worked hard on their research but they have skimped on the job of making their writing clear. This means that readers will have to 'translate' the texts to make sense of the ideas. The only people who will do this are people who have to: colleagues who must keep up with new developments in their field, however badly these are expressed, and students who must read the material on their reading lists. These authors will rarely be read by social scientists outside their speciality, and they will miss the wider audience of educated general readers altogether. This is a pity. Politicians, journalists and active citizens would all be able to do a better job if more writing about the social world were accessible to more people.

We have nagged you about short sentences, finite verbs, the active voice, and clear pronouns, in order to help you improve your writing.

We haven't dwelt on grammar to make students who have problems with English feel inadequate, but to help them get their meaning across more effectively.

Writers who have something to say but expect readers to work hard to find out what it is, are only lazy, not evil. But there are a handful who are obscure on purpose. They do it to be superior, to be fashionable, to impress an in-group that uses the same style, and to hide the mediocrity of their performance. They are counting on no small boys showing up and asking where the emperor's clothes have got to. We should all have freedom of speech but that freedom does not mean that others have to listen to us. We gain an audience's attention by promising to tell them something. If they accept our promise, the right to speak will be matched by the courtesy of a hearing.

It can be hard for novices to know whether they are looking at an author who is lazy, or an author who is clear and considerate but writing about an unfamiliar topic, or an author who is abusing the privilege of print by writing pretentiously about trivia. Think hard before you eliminate the first two possibilities. But if you consider that the third conclusion is justified, don't be afraid to say to so. You don't have to say, 'I think this author is a fake' but you can keep saying, 'I don't understand' until you do. Then you, and the people around you, can judge whether the author is writing about an unfamiliar subject, or is lazy, or is using words to conceal meaning rather than to communicate it. Polite requests for clarity matter; if we are all afraid to say 'I don't understand' we could all end up naked, foolish and impoverished.

In 1970 Popper wrote about a cult of obscurity long-present in German intellectual life, 'the cult of un-understandability'. We don't believe the problem is confined to Germany, and we do find his words worth quoting.

> Many years ago I used to warn my students against the widespread idea that one goes to university in order to learn how to talk, and to write, impressively and incomprehensibly. At the time many students came to university with this ridiculous aim in mind, especially in Germany. And most of those students who, during their university studies, enter into an intellectual climate which accepts this kind of valuation – coming, perhaps under the influence of teachers who in their turn had been reared in a similar climate – are lost. ... One cannot tell truth from falsity, one cannot tell an adequate answer to a problem from an irrelevant one, one cannot tell good ideas from trite ones, one cannot evaluate ideas critically, unless they are presented with sufficient clarity. (1976: 294)

He goes on to say that scholars and social critics should try hard to put their ideas into 'simple, modest language'. This, he says, is an effort 'which those fortunate ones who are able to devote themselves to study owe to society' (1976: 298).

Activities

1. Choose a difficult chapter from one of your textbooks or other assigned readings. Take a page from it and rewrite it. Compare your rewritten version with the original version. What are the differences? What does the page gain by being rewritten?
2. Write two sentences, one using the verb 'affect' and the other using the noun 'effect.'
3. Punctuate the following sentences:
   Shes here and its possible to ask her to help debug Johns program. Its problems arent too hard for her. [Solutions to 3 and 4 are in Appendix 4.]
4. Change the following sentences from the passive to the active voice:
   * It was a warm day; her coat was put in the closet.
   * Ayesha was given a high mark for her essay.
   * The table was surrounded by chairs.
5. Take one of your currently assigned essay topics and brainstorm ideas about it. After brainstorming, write an outline for your essay.

Chapter 8

Numbers

Illustrations

Good writing is clear and concise. It conveys meaning from writer to reader without the reader having to struggle to extract it. Sometimes the best way of conveying meaning is not to rely on words alone but to draw a picture as well. If friends are writing to invite you to stay at their remote beach house it usually helps if they include a map. If we are trying to understand a complex administrative and legal process, such as the procedure for applying for on-shore refugee status in Australia in 2005, a diagram like a flow chart could make the task easier. Clear writing may involve illustrations. These illustrations might be maps or flow charts, or examples of political cartoons or advertisements, but the kind of illustration that you are most likely to use is a table or a graph

Sometimes the clearest way of describing, say, a changing pattern of marriage and divorce, is to provide a table showing the way the rates have moved over a period of time. These tables are not added for ornament. They are not like engravings of the heroine at the ball in a Victorian novel; they are integrated into your text. This means that the words you write discuss the facts you have presented in tabular or graphic form. The text refers to the illustration.

Tables are lists of numbers, and figures are graphs, usually graphs based on tables of numbers. (If you had a map, flow chart, or other kind of diagram you'd call that a 'figure' as well.) Give each illustration a title and, if you are using more than one, number them in sequence. Call your tables 'Table 1', 'Table 2' and so on, and your figures 'Figure 1', 'Figure 2', and so on. This practice means that you can refer to the illustrations succinctly: 'In Table 1 we see … but Figure 3 shows…'

Tables

We will talk about tables taken from secondary sources. Much of the wealth of information available in published sources is expressed in numerical form. Maher and Burke (1991) provide a good idea of some of the official statistics that you can search through for information relevant to your argument. Much of this material is produced by the Australian Bureau of Statistics (ABS). Have a look at their booklet, *Statistics – a Powerful Edge* (1998). You could also consult Betts et al. (2001), especially chapters 3 to 5. But the ABS is not the only source of secondary data. There's a wealth of material available at the Australian Social Science Data Archives at the Australian National University. Some of it is free; in other cases there is a charge. Go to their website and explore <http://assda.anu.edu.au/>.

How should you draw up a table? There are a number of ways in which you can go about this. For example, you may find a table relevant to your argument in a book or article and want to use it, but it contains many numbers. You need not copy it out by hand. Simply photocopy it and paste it into your essay. But give it your own number. Call it 'Table 3', for example, if it's the third table in your essay. You may give it your own title or you can use the title provided by the author. Put the number and the title at the top and then, underneath, provide a reference showing where it came from in just the same way as you would with any other quoted material. (Do not paste in the source given by your source. For example, the author who provided the table may have taken the information from the 2001 census. If you give their reference it will look as if you yourself had consulted the census. Use the author's name, date and page number for your reference.)

...THIS TABLE HASN'T GOT A LEG TO STAND ON...

This cut and paste procedure is acceptable in an undergraduate essay. But the design of a table (like the drawing of a cartoon) is copyright; it belongs to the person who drew the 'illustration' in the first place. If you were writing an official report, or a paper for publication, you should draw up your own table, acknowledging the source of the data but providing your own design. If you wanted to add cartoons or other drawings, you would need permission from the owner of the copyright. (The same is true of photographs unless you took them yourself.)

Perhaps, when you were looking at a table in the secondary literature you decided that you did not need all the detail it provided in order to make your point? For your purposes, the original table contains too much information and so will not provide a clear illustration of the point you want to make. This means you need to redesign the table and to simplify it.

Table 1 gives an example of data taken from two different secondary sources and simplified by omitting some details.

Table 1: School students in Australia—Government and non-government schools, 1964 to 2004 ('000s)

Year	Government	Catholic	Other non-government	Total
1964	1797	463	102	2362
1969	2111	490	112	2712
1974	2253	494	124	2872
1979	2332	513	138	2983
1984	2261	567	190	3018
1989	2194	594	243	3031
1994	2215	602	282	3099
1999	2248	636	343	3227
2004	2260	666	417	3343

Sources: 1963 to 1999 data (Burke and Spaull, 2002: [8]); 2004 data (*Schools*, 2005: 26)
Note: Sub-totals may not add to the exact totals given because of rounding.

Look at the way the table is set out. We have given it plenty of room, separating it from the surrounding text. The number and title are at the top, while the reference to the sources is at the bottom. Each column has a label describing its contents, and so does each row. Each number occupies a 'cell'. We could have ruled up lines for all the rows and all the columns, making a box around every cell. But in a big table like Table 1 this would look black and heavy; artistic considerations play a part.

There is also a note explaining that the totals may not add up exactly to the number given in the 'total' column because of rounding. The figures are in thousands, taken to the nearest one hundred. For example, the number of students in government schools in 1964 was approximately 1 797 000. Burke and Spaull don't tell us the exact number down to the last student. Because the figures have been rounded to the nearest thousand, some years may not add exactly to the total given. They may be 1000 off the mark; for example, the subtotals for 1969 actually add to 2713 and those for 1974 to 2871. (If the totals are one digit out this can be explained by rounding. If the difference is more than one digit a mistake has been made somewhere, or a category has been left out.)

Look again at the title. It describes the contents of the table as accurately as possible. It also shows that the numbers provided are actual numbers (raw figures), not percentages. The expression ('000s) in the title demonstrates this, as well as showing that the numbers are expressed in thousands. We used just a few 'ruled lines' to make the table easier to read. This can be done easily with formatting instructions for tables in a word-processing package, or you can pick up a ruler and do it by hand.

If Table 1 is all you need for your report or essay you could just type the data into a table in a word processing package. But if you thought you might want to present them in other ways as well, it would be a good idea to first type them into a spreadsheet. (You can copy tables from a spreadsheet and paste them into most word processing packages.) Maybe the argument in your essay or report would be clearer if you had a Table 2 which expressed the Table 1 figures as percentages? If you had the numbers already keyed into a spread-sheet you could recalculate them as percentages very quickly. Table 2 shows the data in Table 1 expressed as percentages.

Table 2: School students in Australia—Government and non-government schools, 1964 to 2004 (Percentages)

Year	Government	Catholic	Other non-government	Total
1964	76	20	4	100
1969	78	18	4	100
1974	78	17	4	100
1979	78	17	5	100
1984	75	19	6	100
1989	72	20	8	100
1994	71	19	9	100
1999	70	20	11	100
2004	68	20	12	100

Source: Derived from Table 1
Note: Totals may not add to 100 because of rounding.

The source note has changed. Table 2 is simply derived from Table 1. The note on rounding is similar. (In percentaged tables that have been rounded to the nearest whole number the figures may add to 99, 100 or 101. If you get 98 or 102, there's a mistake somewhere.)

Again, we gave the table plenty of space, and the title and setting out make it clear that this is a table of percentages. Sometimes students feel that it's a waste of space to have a total column just saying 100, 100, 100. It's not. The totals remind readers that they are looking at percentages and they demonstrate the direction in which the numbers have been percentaged. If they were not there, readers might have to puzzle over the table, trying to work out whether down or across was more logical. While they were doing this, the smooth easy flow of communication that you had worked hard to establish would have been broken.

You might draw up Table 1 and put it in your essay to show that enrolments in private schools had increased. But it also shows that all enrolments have increased. Maybe the private schools were just getting a constant share of a larger number? (Though the figures for government schools actually began to decrease after 1979, a reader might not notice this.) Table 2 shows quite clearly that the growth in private school enrolments was not merely a consequence of a growth in overall numbers; enrolments at private schools increased disproportionately.

Figures

You can use figures taken from secondary sources: photocopying relevant graphs and diagrams. But do give them your own number, make sure the title is appropriate for your context and, at the bottom, give the source. Or you may draw a graph yourself. This could be based on statistics you had taken directly from a source, or on statistics that you have derived from the sources.

There are three main types of graph: bar graphs, pie charts and line graphs. Think about the ways in which you could show the data in Table 1 with each of these methods. The statistics could be represented in a line graph, with different coloured lines for each type of school. You would put the years along the 'x' axis and the total numbers of enrolments along the vertical axis (called the 'y' axis). And you would be very careful to show where zero was on your 'y' axis. Look at graphs in newspapers. They often don't show zero. Imagine if we drew a graph of the 'other non-government' enrolments and, instead of beginning our 'y' axis at zero, we started at 102 000. Unless a person read the graph carefully, the numbers would look as if they had begun from almost nothing and then shot up. Line graphs and bar charts must always show zero on the 'y' axis.

If you had keyed all of the numbers for all the years into a spread-sheet you could get the spread-sheet to draw the line graph for you. The program will mark the lines differently for the different types of schools, and if you have a colour printer you can make the final illustration quite attractive.

But you do not have data for all the years, just every five years. So it might be best to chose another kind of graph. What about a pie chart? You can only show one year at a time with these so you would need ten pie charts to represent all the data in Table 1. To do it well you should alter the size of each pie to show the changes in the absolute numbers of enrolments. This looks like hard work. Even if you decided just to select four of five years, the overall result would not be clear. The reason for thinking about a graph in the first place was to improve the reader's picture of the data. Pie charts would not do this. Serious researchers seldom use pie charts.

What about a bar chart? Here you can show the absolute size of each year's enrolments and the numbers in the different types of schools, and you don't have to make any assumptions about a continuous rate of change for the years where you don't have data.

In the following example see how the number of the figure, the title and source note are set out. The categories on the two axes are labelled, and zero is shown clearly. If colours or patterns have been used, a key is provided. If you are drawing your own graphs, include the table, or tables, on which they were based. If you think the tables would be superfluous in the text you can put them into an appendix at the end, and your source note for the graph would then read: 'Source: Derived from Table 1 in Appendix'. (Then, under Table 1 in the appendix, you would give *its* source.)

Figure 1: School students in Australia – Government and non-government schools, 1964 to 2004 ('000s)

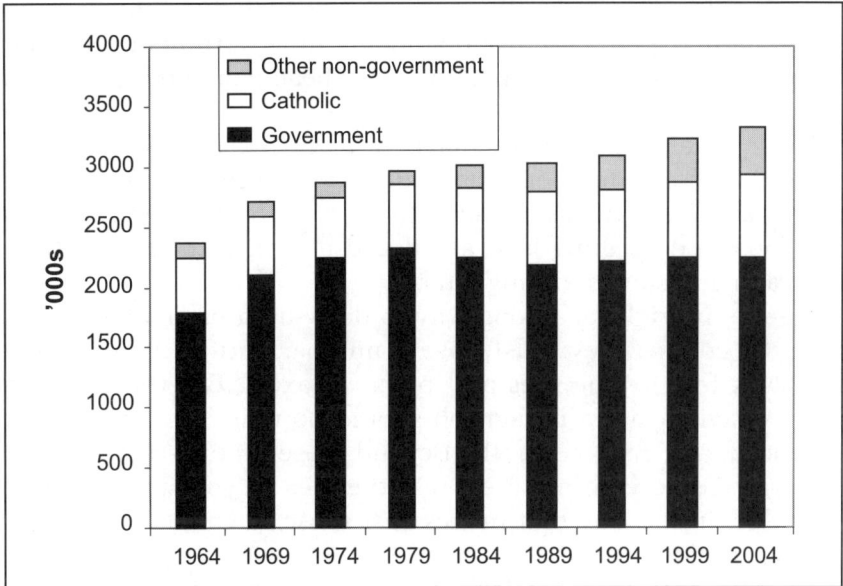

Source: Derived from Table 1

The illustration (table or figure) that you are using in your argument must appear in your text as close as possible to the place where you are referring to it. In this way readers will have the picture of the evidence in front of them, rather than having to scurry backwards and forwards between your text and the appendix. Your reason for producing the illustration, rather than describing the phenomenon in words, was to communicate the facts more clearly. So if you go to the trouble of drawing tables and figures, make sure that they do the work you want them to do.

Writing with numbers

Photocopying tables and figures to paste into your own work is permissible (for students). But it is rather like using a lengthy direct quote. It may be a good quote but it hasn't helped you to learn how to express the ideas in your own words. The table you photocopied may be a good table, well designed and clearly set out, but by picking it up and taking it over wholesale you haven't learned much about expressing your own ideas in your own numbers.

Drawing up a table is much closer to writing a paragraph than it is to doing arithmetic. You have an idea that you want to communicate and you have decided that it would be better to use a table than to use to sentences. We could have put the data in Table 1 into sentences. 'In 1964 there were 1 797 000 students enrolled in Government schools, 463 000 in Catholic schools and 102 000 in other private schools, giving a total of 2 362 000 students. By 1979 the situation had changed. There were 2 332 000 students in Government secondary schools ...' And so on. Imagine how your head would be spinning by the time we got to 2004!

If you have two, three, or maybe four or five numbers, you can get away with putting them into your text in a sentence. But around about four, your reader's capacity to see a pattern in the numerical facts you are describing is strained and it is time to stop writing a paragraph and start planning a table.

There is no right or wrong way to draw up a particular table or figure. Of course, they must have a number, a title, a source note and labels for the columns and rows (or axes). But that's just the same as saying that a paragraph should be written grammatically, referenced, and spelt correctly. Beyond these ground-rules, you are in charge. You are going to express the idea in your paragraph, or your table, in the way that makes best sense to you as you develop your argument.

Look at Table 1 again. Perhaps you want to emphasise changes over time. Would it be better to put the years across the top and the types of schools down the side? Perhaps you want to emphasise Catholic schools. Should you combine the figures for government and other non-government schools and just have two sub-total columns, Catholic and other? Or maybe you could print the Catholic sub-totals in bold (or print them in red ink)? Perhaps you only really need the figures for 1984 and 1989 because you are interested in the possible effects of the 1987 stock market crash on private school enrolments? In Table 2, should you round to the nearest whole number (as we have done), or do you need more detail? Should you take the numbers to one decimal point or two?

We can't tell you the correct way to write a paragraph about changes in school enrolments because we don't know what you want to say about them. We can only give general advice such as: 'Write clearly and document your sources.' It's the same with tables and figures. Write clearly, document your sources, and use the illustration to say what you want to say. In other words, use it to demonstrate the features of the variable (or variables) that interest you.

Variables and the unit of analysis

What is a variable? Just about everything. Or, rather, just about everything can be a variable, according to the way we want to think about it. A variable is a concept (like total school enrolments, or ethnic background, or age, or social class) which can take on different values: enrolments can be higher or lower, people can be older or younger, and their class or ethnic background may not be the same. In Chapter 4 we thought about writing an essay on the variable of fertility. In Chapter 6 we dealt with a research report on the relationship between the variables 'attitudes to attempts at religious conversion' and 'pre-existing belief systems', and the sample essay in Appendix 1 discusses a number of concepts (power, paradigms, dogma, humanism, empiricism) which could all be treated as variables.

We have been talking about variables all along, but it seems sensible to introduce them in an explicit way here in this chapter. When researchers are drawing up tables they can't help but become aware of the fact that almost all of their concepts can be thought of as variables. In 1964 there were 2 362 000 children and young people enrolled in Australian schools. By 2004 total enrolments had changed. The variable had varied. So the concept of 'total school enrolments' is not fixed. Think about ethnic background. It may not be a variable as far as an individual is concerned. A person may say: 'I'm French and that's that; a leopard doesn't change its spots.' But even if this is true for the individual, the ethnicity of suburbs and states and nations can change, and so can the age structure of an area, or its typical composition in terms of social class. If the focus of our study is a geographical area rather than a person, all of these concepts are potential variables. When the focus of attention is individual people, ethnicity and class can be important variables even if they do not change within any one person. Social scientists are always interested in more than one individual and the range of people they study may differ, or vary, in terms of class, ethnicity, age, gender and other characteristics.

If you are writing with words you may not need to devote conscious thought to the question: 'What are the central variables here?' You just write about them. But it does help to be a little more self-conscious when drawing up a table. Ask yourself two questions: what is my key variable (or variables) and what is my focus of attention? Is it geographic areas, individuals or something else? When you are looking for an answer to that second question (what is my focus of attention?), you are concentrating on the problem of the unit of analysis. Look at Table 1 again. It tells us that in 1964 there were

2 362 000 somethings enrolled in Australian schools. Ask yourself: 'What is one something?' Answer: 'It's one school student.' The unit of analysis in Table 1 is one person. Look at Table 3.

Table 3: Motor Vehicle Ownership: Melbourne Statistical Division (MSD) and selected Local Government Areas, 1986 (percentages)

% of households with:	MSD	St Kilda	Footscray	Springvale	Melton
no vehicle	13.2	34.5	26.9	9.4	3.5
1 vehicle	40.4	48.1	48.5	41.2	38.8
2 vehicles	35.0	14.4	19.2	37.1	46.7
3+ vehicles	11.3	2.9	5.3	12.2	11.1
Total	**100.0**	**100.0**	**100.0**	**100.0**	**100.0**

Source: *Melbourne: Facts and Figures* (n.d.: 107, 57, 115, 81)
Note: Totals may not add to 100.0 because of rounding

What is the unit of analysis here? A Local Government Area? A vehicle? Or a household? The table contains information about the percentages of some things. In the first cell (in the top left) we have the figure showing that 13.2 per cent in the MSD have no vehicle. Ask yourself: '13.2 per cent of what?' The answer is 13.2 per cent of households. So the unit of analysis in Table 3 is one household.

To draw up a useful table you need to know what variable (or variables) you are describing and you need to know your unit of analysis. It will usually be one person, but it can be something else. When you know that it is something else you will be able to design a table that shows this to the reader as clearly as possible. We have tried to do this with the heading for the rows: '% of households with:'. Maybe we could have made it even clearer by altering the title to something like 'Motor Vehicle Ownership in households...'

(Look at the source note. There was no date of publication printed in the book from which we got the figures. This is rare with a published source but it can happen. You indicate this by using 'n.d.' for 'no date'.)

One variable or two?

Tables and graphs are another way of writing but they are also a way of drawing. They provide us with a way of drawing pictures of ideas, ideas that would be hard to describe in words alone. Writers become artists whenever adding a picture gets their meaning across more effectively. You learnt the basics for drawing pictures of ideas expressed in numbers at primary school when you mastered adding, subtracting, multiplying and dividing. Adding up and calculating percentages took you a long way then, and they will go on to do so at university. But you will need to think about something further. Are you drawing a picture of changes in one variable or are you looking at two at once? It's a bit like the difference between drawing a flat design (like a map) or showing a street scene in perspective.

So far we have presented tables that show changes in one variable: school enrolments over time and vehicle ownership in different places. (When we look at one variable by itself we call this 'univariate analysis'.) But what if you wanted to look at one variable in terms of another? What if you wanted to know the educational background of the parents who sent their children to the different types of schools, or the income of the households with no vehicles and those with three or more? If you are looking at one variable in terms of another you are doing bivariate analysis; this means you are looking at two variables at once. Table 4 gives us information about the variable of employment status and the variable of gender.

Table 4: Labour force by gender, Australia, civilian labour force aged 15 plus, February 2005 ('000s)

Labour force status	Males	Females	Total persons
Employed	5451.5	4429.8	9881.3
Unemployed	281.0	245.2	526.2
Total labour force	**5732.4**	**4675.1**	**10 407.5**

Source: *Australian Labour Market Statistics* (2005: 37)

Many bivariate tables look like Table 4. Think of it as a classic two-by-two format. It's called a 'two-by-two' table because the cells we are really interested in are the four shaded ones in the centre. (We've shaded them to help you see why it's called a two-by-two table. You wouldn't normally do this, because shading makes the numbers harder to read.)

You could make the table more complex by dividing the employment status variable into part-time and full-time, or by including the category, 'not in the labour force', but it's often useful to begin by thinking of your bivariate analysis in as simple a form as possible. (For example, if you had data on vehicle ownership by household income you could start by sketching a table which showed the number of vehicles owned as either 'none' or 'some' and household income simply as 'high' and 'low'.)

The unit of analysis in Table 4 is one person and the table shows us raw figures in thousands. What should we do if we wanted to show the data as percentages? Obviously we should express the raw figures as a percentage of 'the total' but the table gives us not one total but five. First there are the row and column totals. These are called 'marginals'. They show: total men; total women; total employed people; and total unemployed people. Then there is a grand total. Which of the five should we use?

Before you can answer this question you need to know something else. You need to know the difference between a dependent variable and an independent variable. This sounds like jargon; let us interpret. Roughly speaking, an independent variable is a variable that you think may be working as a cause, and a dependent variable is a variable that you think may be being affected by that cause. Thus household income (independent variable) may affect vehicle ownership (dependent variable).

Why don't we just say 'cause' and 'effect'? The reason for using the unfamiliar terms, 'independent' and 'dependent' variables, is that we don't want to commit ourselves before we have more information. Maybe something else other than household income is the real cause of the number of vehicles owned? (Distance from public transport perhaps, or number of the people in the household? Perhaps all three combine as causes?) The term 'independent variable' allows us to say that we are treating a variable as if it might be the cause without committing ourselves to the conclusion that it really is the cause.

As long as we are imagining that household income affects vehicle ownership we are treating it as an independent variable. In the same way we are often interested in the gender (or age, or educational attainment) of employed and unemployed people because we think that gender or age or education may have some effect on the likelihood of a person finding a job.

When we do bivariate analysis we are playing with the idea that one variable may have a causal effect on another variable. In Table 4 gender is the independent variable and employment status is the dependent variable. It's certainly an oversimplification to say that gender might cause unemployment. Obviously unemployment has many causes. But it is not unreasonable to imagine that something about gender might have some effect on a person's labour force status. (In contrast, think of it the other way around. It would be silly to pretend that a person's employment status might affect their gender.)

When we percentage a bivariate table we always percentage it in the direction of the independent variable. You look at the unemployed men as a percentage of all men in the labour force and the unemployed women as a percentage of all women in the labour force. In this way you can compare the men and the women and see if gender really does seem to make a difference to the likelihood of a person being unemployed.

Table 5: Labour force by gender, Australia, civilian labour force aged 15 plus, February 2005 (percentages)

Labour force status	Males	Females	Total persons
Employed	95.1	94.8	94.9
Unemployed	4.9	5.2	5.1
Total labour force	100.0	100.0	100.0
Total N ('000s)	5732.4	4675.1	10 407.5

Source: Derived from Table 4
Note: Totals may not add to 100 because of rounding.

Table 5 suggests that gender does not have much effect on whether a person is likely to be employed or unemployed. In February 2005, women were just slightly more likely to be unemployed than men, but the difference was tiny. We could not have discovered this if we had worked out the raw figures as a percentage of the grand total because there were more men than women in the grand total. And we certainly could not have discovered it if we had first worked out the employed men as a percentage of all employed people, the employed women as a percentage of all employed people, and then the unemployed men as a percentage of all unemployed people and the unemployed women as a percentage of all unemployed people. Percentaging in the direction of the dependent variable gets you nowhere. Never do it. Percentaging in the direction of the grand total is almost always just as useless. This leaves us with the golden rule: if you are doing bivariate analysis, percentage in the direction of the independent variable.

Table 6 is a little more complex; it gives a fuller picture of working life by gender.

Table 6: Labour-force status and participation in the labour force, by gender, Australia, civilian population aged 15 plus, February 2005 (percentages)

Labour force status	Males	Females	Total persons
Employed full-time	58.1	29.5	43.6
Employed part-time	10.3	24.3	17.4
Unemployed	3.5	3.0	3.2
Not in the labour force	28.0	43.2	35.7
Total	100.0	100.0	100.0
Total N ('000s)	**7995.8**	**8257.5**	**16 253.3**

Source: *Australian Labour Market Statistics* (2005: 37–40)
Note: The percentage unemployed is not calculated as a proportion of the labour force, as is usual, but as a percentage of the civilian population aged 15 plus.
Totals may not add to 100 because of rounding.

Table 6 alters the picture about unemployment and gender that we got from Table 5; here women are less likely to be unemployed than men. (This is because there are more women aged 15 plus overall than there are men. So the number of unemployed women now forms a smaller percentage of the larger total.) But it also shows that women are more likely to work part-time and more likely not to be in the labour force at all than men. Note the length of the title. Sometimes you need a lot of words to differentiate a new table from a previous one and to describe its contents accurately. There is also a note explaining that the normal convention of expressing the unemployed as a percentage of the labour force (people with work plus people looking for work) has not been followed.

We get a more fine-grained picture of working life by gender from Table 6, but the table is still percentaged in the direction of the independent variable. Did you read the story of Tootle the Train in the 'Little Golden Books' when you were young? Tootle was a young engine who liked to slip off the railway tracks and chase butterflies in the meadow. This caused his engine driver and the people of the local town much anxiety. They joined forces to teach him a serious lesson, to teach him the virtue of the golden rule: 'Staying on the rails no matter what.' You need to learn the golden rule: 'Always percentage in the direction of the independent variable.' Remember this and, like Tootle, you will go on to lead a useful and contented life.

We percentage in the direction of the independent variable because this is the only way of seeing whether this presumed 'causal factor' does indeed have some effect on the dependent variable. If there were no effect the percentages in the sub-total columns for men and women would be the same as the 'marginal' percentages in the column for all persons.

Percentaging in the direction of the independent variable is the only logical thing to do, but bivariate tables have at least two other features which are more a matter of convention than logic. The title is arranged according to the formula 'dependent variable *by* independent variable', in this case, 'Labour-force status ... *by* gender'. And the independent variable is usually set out along the top of the table while the dependent variable is down the side. When you are reading a table you may ask yourself: What is this writer's independent variable? It's the variable slotted in after the word 'by'. Then you can do a second quick check. Is this variable set out across the top of the table? Yes. Writers do not have to observe these conventions, but if they do they make it easier for readers to grasp their meaning.

Going further with statistics?

If you are interested in learning more about analysing statistical data, see: de Vaus (2002); Foddy (1988); Bouma (2004); and Betts et al. (2001). Gonick and Smith (1993), *The Cartoon Guide to Statistics*, is a cheerful and comprehensive book, though novices will need help from tutors or knowledgeable friends if they are to follow it through to the end and be able, as the authors claim they should be, 'to do anything with statistics, except lie, cheat, steal and gamble'.

These, and other introductory books on analysing and presenting data contain basic information on univariate and bivariate analysis. Some (like de Vaus, Foddy, and Gonick and Smith) take their readers well beyond this basic introductory material. But as an undergraduate student, you are more likely to need to understand sophisticated statistics for some of your reading than for your own writing. A few of the books and articles that you come across will refer to advanced statistics and it is frustrating not to be able to follow authors who rely on these, and thus not to be able to assess their work. Most undergraduate research projects, and many postgraduate ones, do not call for advanced statistics. If you are presenting numerical data, simple tables and figures will take you a long way and these usually only need primary school arithmetic. Your skills as a writer and a designer will be far more important here than any genius you may have for mathematics.

Activity

Assume that you are doing a research project on the effects of economic restructuring in manufacturing industries on the employment of male migrants in Australia in the 1980s. You think that migrants would have been more heavily affected by restructuring than Australian-born workers. This is because you have a hypothesis that migrant men were more likely to have been employed in manufacturing industries than native-born men. You have gathered the following data from the 1986 Census:

- Number of men in employment: 3 951 903
- Number of overseas-born men in employment: 1 036 918
- Number of men working in manufacturing industries: 714 351
- Number of overseas-born men working in manufacturing industries: 250 226.

(Source: *Census 86 – Cross-Classified Characteristics*, 1986: 121, 122)

Use these data to construct a two-by-two table to test the hypothesis that migrant men are more likely to be employed in manufacturing industries than the native-born men. After you have made a serious attempt at the exercise, turn to Appendix 4 for a sample solution where you can check your work against ours. Hint: you will need two tables, one for the raw data and a final one to show the percentaged data.

Two-by-two tables are a useful way to start any bivariate analysis. Draw up the framework you think you will need and worry about the numbers afterwards. The arithmetic is simple. The brain work lies in planning what the final table will look like.

Chapter 9

Handing it in and getting it back

Objectives
➤ To learn how to present essays and research reports
➤ To learn your rights as a student
➤ To learn the criteria you will be assessed against

Outline
➤ The final draft
➤ Presentation
➤ Students' rights
➤ Assessment criteria
➤ Getting the work back and getting better

The final draft

Aim to get a semi-final draft completed a week before the essay is due so you can revise with a fresh eye. This goal may be unattainable if multiple essays are due thick and fast but, if you plan for a week's grace to allow for revision, you will at least have that week in reserve when the unexpected happens and you fall behind.

We hope you will have time to do major surgery on your argument if it seems necessary when you come back to it with that fresh eye. But at the least check the length of your sentences, check your pronouns, and make sure your presentation meets the expected standard. It won't help for your first essay but, for all subsequent ones, re-read comments on previous essays. Check that you have not repeated any mistakes that were picked up earlier.

Proofread and correct typing errors. Check the referencing in your text. Have you provided a reference for every quote, direct or indirect, and for every statement of fact that is not absolutely common knowledge?

If you are using the author/date system, does every work cited by you as a reference in your text also appear in your list of references at the end and *vice versa*? (If you are using numbered footnotes, all sources should also be listed in a final list of references.) Is the form of your referencing correct? Have you supplied a title page? If you have referred to an appendix (or appendices) in the text is it included with the document you are handing in?

Always keep a copy. With computer files, keep a backup. If you don't have an extra hard copy, keep two backups. It happens very rarely, but an essay can get lost before it's marked. This is a tragedy if you have no copy. Or it can be lost after it's marked. This is also serious because, while you will know your grade, you will not get the detailed comments that your tutor will have written on the text. Indeed, if you do not have a copy you will soon have difficulty remembering what you said. Good essays are more often lost after they are marked than poor ones. They are stolen by worms in the academic woodwork looking for material to plagiarise. Ask about the arrangements for handing essays back. If it is the end of the semester and they have to be left in some semi-public spot for students to pick up, ask if you can submit yours with a stamped addressed envelope and have it posted to you. (Sometimes the arrangement will be that you must submit an envelope. If you don't, your tutor may not provide comments on your work – it is a waste of their time to write comments that won't be read.)

With research reports, especially research reports based on primary analysis, keep all your working documents until the report has been assessed and returned. This means that, if you are called in for an interview to explain aspects of your report, you will be able to produce these documents to show how you arrived at your results. (On the few unhappy occasions where a student may be suspected of manufacturing data the evidence provided by working papers will be important. If you have kept working documents for essays you will be able to substantiate your authorship if this should be questioned.)

Word limits and deadlines were discussed in Chapter 2. Most tutors will not be put out if you are a couple of hundred words either side of the word limit, but deadlines are more serious. You should be able to complete your plan showing when each essay is due at the beginning of the semester. You need this plan so that you can organise your time. If you don't have the information to put it together somebody (not you) is not pulling their weight. See the section on 'students' rights' below.

Presentation

There are hard aspects of essay writing and easy aspects. Working out your ideas and expressing them clearly can be difficult and time-consuming. It's a shame if a student endangers the final product by handing in a pile of tattered sheets of paper, scratched over with unreadable handwriting, tied up with string and looking as if they had been slept on for a week. Not only is this poor impression management, it is also a waste of time because the tutor will hand it back and ask for it to be re-submitted.

Specific requirements can differ in different departments, so check to see if there are variations that you should note. But if you follow the suggestions below, you are unlikely to be reproved for poor presentation.

- Write on one side of the paper only.
- All your margins (top, bottom, left and right) should be at least 2.5 cm.
- Provide a title page setting out your name, the essay topic in full, your tutorial time, day and hour, and your tutor's name. (Big departments may employ many tutors; you need to make sure that your essay gets to the right person.)
- List your references on a separate page (or pages) at the end of your essay.
- Indent new paragraphs and leave a space between them.
- Your essay printout should be double spaced (except for the indented quotes). This means there should be a blank line in between each line of text. If you don't double space, your tutor won't have room to make comments or corrections.
- Number the pages.

Look at the sample documents in Appendices 1 and 2. Except for the fact that they are printed on both sides of the paper and are single-spaced to save space they follow these suggestions.

The final document represents a lot of work. We sympathise with students who want to protect their essays by putting them into stout folders, but these folders make the essay difficult to open out and read. Your tutor will probably have to take it out of the folder and hunt round for a stapler to keep the pages together. It's best to staple the pages yourself (in the top left hand corner only). Most tutors prefer it if you submit your assignments without any extra adornments.

Students' rights

This book is full of advice about the steps students ought to take and the procedures they should follow to produce interesting and acceptable written papers. We hope you find your work rewarding but there's no denying that the student role is full of shoulds and oughts, of duties and responsibilities. However you do have rights as well and these should be respected.

- You have a right to a subject hand-out at the beginning of the semester. This should show the topics to be covered each week, list some introductory reading material for them, and explain the assessment. The notes on assessment should show the per cent of the total marks for the subject that each piece is worth. They should also show the dates when each piece is due.
- You have the right to receive each essay question (or research assignment) well before its due date.
- You have a right to written details about the style of presentation required, including the style of the referencing system you are to use.
- You have a right to have written comments on your work as well as a grade. (This applies to essays and research reports that you prepare and hand in. Simple fact tests, or formal exams, usually only get a grade.)
- You have a right to have a properly qualified person read your work and mark it carefully. And you have a right to know who this person is.
- If you have difficulty understanding the comments, you have a right to talk to the person who marked your paper so that you can work out what you should do to improve the next essay or report.

If you feel that your rights have been breached, speak up. Try to talk to the person immediately responsible first. Perhaps it's a misunderstanding or an oversight. If talking does not resolve the problem go higher up, to the subject coordinator, the head of department or the dean. If this seems a bit scary, go to the student union to check that you do have a case and to get moral support.

We have met students who do not work hard and who do not fill their part of the academic bargain. We also know that, occasionally, a few teachers do not fill their part either. Students who have been short-changed should complain.

Assessment criteria

When you have handed the essay in it is launched. You have done your best and you know what the person marking it is looking for: a clear argument well-grounded in the evidence, relevant to the question, and properly documented and presented. Here is a summary of the criteria readers use when they are marking essays and reports.

- Relevance. Did this student answer the question (or fulfil the research brief)?

- Argument. Is the argument clear and logical and is it a good argument? Are key concepts well-defined? Good arguments are supported by evidence but they also represent the student's original thinking. How else could an argument be constructed?
- Reading. Is the breadth of reading appropriate for the task?
- Expression. Is the work clearly and grammatically expressed? If numerical data are included, can the student use numbers to support and express ideas?
- Presentation. Is the form of the referencing correct? This is the most important part of presentation. But the points listed above under 'presentation' also count. Is this essay or report clearly set out so that the tutor has no difficulty in reading and assessing it?

Getting the work back and getting better

We all want praise. It feels better than corrections. Good essays deserve praise but, if you want the next one to be even better, appreciate the corrections as well. Don't feel that the corrections mean you are inadequate. Most academics know that their own work can be improved if someone else reads it and offers suggestions or corrections. The process of being corrected doesn't stop when you reach some magic plateau of perfection; getting feedback and learning how to use it constructively is part of writing. You are trying to improve your skills in a world where no one, not even the person marking your work, is perfect.

Tutors try to write comments in a constructive spirit, but they also write them to justify the grade they have given and the cumulative effect of this can feel like disapproval. Implicitly, the tutor is saying, 'This essay is a fair attempt but it gets a C rather than a B+ because...' This is followed by a list of all the improvements that the student could have made if they had wanted to write a better essay and get a higher mark. Many tutors also try to provide ideas for improvement even for very good essays. It is hard for a student to learn from feedback that simply says: 'Well done!'

When we came home from primary school with a bright and splashy painting, or a tough grade-three reader finished, or the class chess championship in our bag, the family went into raptures. But they did this because we were children, children who needed lashings of praise and encouragement. Now we are grown up. When another adult gives you considered feedback they are paying you a compliment. They are saying: 'I take your work so seriously that I feel it's worthwhile thinking hard about ways in which you could improve it.' In the grown-up world, 'Yes, dear, very nice' is not a compliment.

Everyone finds the transition from unstinted praise to careful criticism painful. The sooner we can adjust to it the sooner we will be able to master the sophisticated subject matter and advanced skills of university subjects. Once they are mastered, we can use them creatively. Developing an argument and grounding it in the evidence involves many skills, and so does accumulating sources, writing clearly and presenting data. All skills improve with practice and feedback. Practice alone won't do it. Imagine learning to sing by yourself, with no one to tell you how it sounds.

Feedback is important and so is learning to appreciate good examples of the work you'd like to be able to do yourself. Apprentice singers listen to trained voices; they model themselves on the best. Apprentice writers in the social sciences have a handicap; they have to read some material written by people who write poorly. Not all of the role models are opera stars. But apprentice social scientists can at least learn to tell the good from the bad, the clear and comprehensible from the lazy and conceited, and to acquire the confidence to base their own decisions on their own judgement.

Students who are learning the methods of the reasoned argument are being initiated into a new culture. Alvin Gouldner calls it the culture of careful and critical discourse (1979: 28–30). Almost everyone who has influence in social policy, government, business, politics, the serious media and academic life are part of this culture. You, as you progress through your course, are being invited to join it too. We hope that the transition from the outside to the inside gives more pleasure than pain and that you will use the culture of careful and critical discourse, not just within the circle of those who know and understand its rules, but in the wider world with whatever you choose to do afterwards.

Appendix 1

Sample essay

Subject: AS204 Social Theory
Semester 2: 2005
South Eastern University

Analyse the main themes expressed by C. Wright Mills in his book *The Sociological Imagination* and briefly evaluate the contribution it has made to sociology.

Name: Kerry Brice*
Tutor: Michael Bosswick*
Tutorial: Friday 2 pm., Room BA1002

C. Wright Mills and *The Sociological Imagination*

In this essay I will discuss two themes in *The Sociological Imagination*: the moral criterion of relevance and the question of the relationship between values and power. The two themes are interconnected. Mills shows that to concentrate on 'values' and ignore the historical structures of power in a community is to evade the social scientists' responsibility. Their responsibility, their purpose, is to make structures explicit, and thereby help individuals understand their private troubles in terms of public issues.

> In the introduction the student says what she's going to say and do in the essay.

I will also consider the implications of Mills's themes for the practice of sociology, asking whether he has provided sociology with a paradigm in the sense in which the word is used by Thomas Kuhn.[1] A paradigm is like a broad and general theory, but a general theory that has gained widespread acceptance among the community of scholars. It defines what it is possible to know and how it is possible to arrive at knowledge; it defines what is scientific and what is speculative or metaphysical. For Kuhn the determining characteristic of scientific communities is that they hold paradigms in common.[2] Has Mills provided an outline of the field of inquiry to be investigated by sociologists? Has he laid down the methodological rules by which research should proceed within that field of inquiry? Or, to use Kuhn's terminology, has Mills provided the discipline with rules for the practice of 'normal science',[3] rules for careful and systematic work on the puzzles (the potentially soluble problems) suggested by that paradigm? Through an analysis of his themes of morality and power, I will argue that although we cannot separate values from the practice of sociology, we must not take this to mean that useful social research is not possible.

> Notice how the student defines her terms as she goes along.

> The last sentence tells us to expect this analysis in the following sections.

Morality

> The sub-heading tells us that we are shifting to the body of the essay.

Mills says that the social sciences must consider public issues and private troubles, and the relationship between the two. This is their promise and their task.[4] The platform on which he develops this moral imperative consists, in the beginning, of a denunciation of the ways in which it has been evaded.

---

[1] See T.S. Kuhn, *The Structure of Scientific Revolutions*, University of Chicago Press, Chicago, 1970, p.10.
[2] ibid., p.19.
[3] ibid., pp.5, 35 ff.
[4] C.W. Mills, *The Sociological Imagination*, Penguin, Harmondsworth, 1970, p.12.

So we have Grand Theory and abstracted empiricism, two differing modes of evasion. By 'Grand Theory' Mills is referring to the work of Talcott Parsons. He sees this work as seeking to construct a conceptual system that will explain the nature of all societies in all times. He finds the attempt absurd. Grand Theory is marked not just by pretentious mannerisms, but by contradictions that become implicit when it takes off from the real empirical world. Grand Theory, flying high above historical structures, makes a sky geometry of social systems and social values. Builders of these trans-historical systems arbitrarily limit themselves to the 'social', a term which for them excludes politics and economics, and so excludes many of the structures of power. An area is cornered off for sociology on the negative grounds that no other discipline has appropriated it already. When the pioneers were developing a sociological consciousness, this kind of thinking may have been excusable, but to shrink back behind limits is now quite cowardly and far from Grand.[5] How can a universal system be built on such a restricted conventional base? How, too, can such a system be built without empirical content?

Mills enjoys his exposé of the high-flying naked emperor, but the abstracted empiricist, small Earth dweller with the methodologically crossed eyes, is a more serious foe. (Why 'abstracted'? The image evoked is of epistemologists, or absent-minded professors, rather than *selective* empiricists.) People of this type are more dangerous because their pretensions are scientific rather than Grand.

Mills' attack on abstracted empiricism has a parallel in Matthew Arnold's *Literature and Dogma*. In the nineteenth century, religion felt itself besieged by science, its authority undermined by the prestige of scientific method. Some theologians retaliated with dogma; they defined faith very exactly and made logical deductions from these dogmatic premises. Arnold felt that religion should be interpreted in a literary way, as part of a cultural tradition;[6] to do otherwise alienated ordinary people and rendered the religious message absurd.[7]

Mills has set himself a similar critical task in this century. The taunt that sociologists ape science in a ridiculous way[8] is justified inasmuch as they build foolish scientific superstructures on an inappropriate base. Sociology should be a humanistic attempt to understand people and society, an attempt to grasp history and

5 ibid., pp.44–47.
6 M. Arnold, *Literature and Dogma,* Ungar, New York, 1970, p.9.
7 ibid., p.21 ff.
8 C.W. Mills, 'Introduction', in C.W. Mills (Ed.), *Images of Man: The Classical Tradition in Sociological Thinking*, Braziller, New York, 1960, p.1.

biography and the relationship between the two.[9] This provides the goal of the discipline and the terms of reference within which it should be judged.

For Mills, 'social research of any kind is advanced by ideas: it is only disciplined by fact'.[10] His edict holds for historical studies as well as contemporary surveys. Hypotheses are checked and documented at key points; to attempt more than this is to stifle the effort to understand.

The Grand Theorist hides his lack of empirical reference with pretentious language; the abstracted empiricist conceals his lack of conceptual guidelines with methodological camouflage. Both schools are engaged in ensuring that we do not learn too much about people and society.[11]

As the Grand Theorist shakes the facts out of his scheme, the abstracted empiricist claims to have shaken the values out of his facts. While Mills is attacking the abstracted empiricists' claim to be operating in a value-free manner he is, in effect, accusing them of labouring under the fallacy of induction.[12] He is accusing them of a naive failure to appreciate that so-called 'value-free' facts can only be perceived if we already have some sort of perspective, some pre-existing theoretical ideas about the world. All world views, the scientific and the everyday, are selective. As Kuhn puts it:

> ...something like a paradigm is prerequisite to perception itself. What a man sees depends both upon what he looks at and also upon what his previous visual-conceptual experience has taught him to see.[13]

It is not possible for interpretation to rise up from neutral data, because neutral data do not and cannot exist. They have been selected and gathered, often with difficulty, with some end in view. The facts may or may not be hard, but no-one can see and collect them all. If theory is not explicit it must be implicit.

Like the Grand Theorist, the value-free empiricists stand on ironically false ground. In the empiricists' case this is because their neutral scientism is most often hired out to bureaucracy, the bureaucracy of government, the military establishment and industry. It has become integrated into, rather than critical of, the manipulative modern epoch.[14] Perhaps of its nature, it could not do otherwise. It requires an army of technicians, a reservoir of money.

---

[9] Mills, 1970, op. cit., pp.12, 192.
[10] ibid., p. 82.
[11] ibid., 86.
[12] ibid., pp.76–78.
[13] Kuhn, op. cit., p.113.
[14] Mills, 1970, op. cit., pp.106, 116–120.

Who will fuel this machine for no reward?

Mills does not argue that it is impossible to practise an independent social science. Rather he claims that sociology in the classic tradition does not require administrative machinery. Its tradition is one of individual scholarship and intellectual craftsmanship, concerned above all with historical structures and their relationships with individuals.[15]

How does this tradition operate, and what should it be doing?

Values and Power

Mills uses a puzzling concept in his introduction to the *Images of Man*. It can, I think, illuminate the dual theme of *The Sociological Imagination*. He says that sociology is faced by a twofold crisis: the retreat into the supposed neutrality of fact and the terrifying intersection of culture and politics.[16] The supposed neutrality of fact, the retreat from issues behind a screen of 'science', this is not difficult to understand. But the 'terrifying intersection of culture and politics', what can this mean?

Perhaps the phrase may be interpreted something like this: values come from the powerful, or at least are shaped by them. If values determine power, why should this be terrifying? If impartial goodness and disinterested virtue always guided laws, bureaucracies and armies we might be puzzled, but not afraid. But this, Mills implies, does not happen. People's values, their ideas of what is good and what is virtuous, are shaped by the powerful, in the interests of the powerful. So why conduct numerous unconnected surveys of opinion and belief? These are the results of structure, not the determinants. They are symptoms not causes. If you put sociology in a separate box, labelled, say, 'values and interaction', separate from politics and economics and isolated in the microcosm of the present, you will be left with these results, this collection of symptoms, and you will have no way of finding out what they mean.

If we only look at the values people profess we will not understand. The picture must be seen whole, with no arbitrary limitations. Hence Mills' two-edged attack on Grand Theory and abstracted empiricism: the one produces cloudy concepts about common values, the other measures them in the limited circumstances of milieux.[17] Neither care where they come from or what they mean.

---

[15] See ibid., pp. 215–248.

[16] Mills, 1960, op. cit., p.9.

[17] Mills, 1970, op. cit., p.86.

> This links the previous section with the next one, providing a nice segue.

> Here the author links the current material with her ideas from the previous section, elaborating them.

Mills sees ideas and values as the legitimations of structure, not as causes.[18] Taken at this general level, his perspective is consistent with either of two main theoretical positions on ideology. It is consistent either with the position that subordinate classes are indoctrinated by an ideology formed in the interests of the dominant classes, or with the position that holds that some, or all, of the beliefs of subordinate groups are a product of their structural situation. Ideas are formed in response to the pressures that they (and we) are subjected to as a part of daily living.[19] In neither case does it make sense to see prevailing patterns of belief and opinion as having a causal autonomy of their own that can be understood without looking at history and the structures of power.

The sociological imagination should try to make historical structures explicit and, by so doing, clarify their effects on the individuals who make up society.[20] This conception of the sociologist's task does not imply that people are the pawns of social forces, for they have the potential to understand and evaluate their circumstances and to bring about change.[21] But to realise this potential, they need the help of the sociological imagination. If social scientists withhold this help by affecting a neutral, 'apolitical' stance, they ally themselves with dehumanising and destructive forces. Are they in the business of helping people solve private troubles by explaining them in terms of public issues? Or are they bureaucrats concerned with the maintenance of military and industrial power?

Paradigms and Social Science

The Sociological Imagination is a moral book: it presents moral choices in the strongest terms. These are not the kind of choices which can be resolved by proof. To accept or reject them is to accept or reject a conversion experience. Kuhn, in *The Structure of Scientific Revolutions*, has shown us that emotional, extra-rational choices are not the prerogative of the arts or religion, but are central to the progress of natural science. Thus the most empirical of social scientists need not shrink from entertaining them.

We can look at the goals Mills sets for contemporary social science through Kuhn's idea of the paradigm, the common way in which scientists agree to perceive their field. A paradigm outlines what it is possible to know and how it

In the next section the author solidifies and clarifies her argument. She refers back to the evidence she presented in the previous sections and uses it to make her point.

---

[18] ibid., p.48.
[19] See C. Chamberlain, *Class Consciousness in Australia*, Allen and Unwin, Sydney, 1983, pp.1–12.
[20] Mills, 1970, op. cit., pp.188–191.
[21] ibid., pp. 192–195.

is possible to arrive at knowledge; it is both a map and instructions for map-making.[22] We can, I think, apply Kuhn more widely, for a paradigm need not be 'scientific' in any narrow sense. Indeed, Kuhn says 'scientific' may not mean anything more than something which possesses a common paradigm, and by virtue of this makes cumulative progress. (What counts as 'progress' is defined by the paradigm.)[23] For example, Dr Spock provided a generation of parents with a child rearing paradigm. The most important characteristic of a paradigm is that it provides a community with a commonly accepted definition of their field of interest. When this is achieved, the members of the community can confidently fall to work.

So if, as Mills says, all in the social sciences is chaos, schism and confusion, if arguments about method inhibit constructive work, if practitioners cannot even agree about the nature of social science,[24] then the field fits Kuhn's description of an area of study still in a 'pre-paradigmatic' stage.[25] This means that sociology is not yet a science (a discipline which can make rapid cumulative progress) because, though individuals and schools are concerned about a common set of phenomena, they have not yet adopted a common way of looking at these phenomena. They have not yet agreed to accept a common paradigm as an outline map of their field.

To say 'have not yet' is to assume that, in time, a generally accepted paradigm will be achieved. But 'pre-paradigmatic', like 'pre-Christian' and 'pre-Romantic' is a label that can only be applied in retrospect. To use it of social science as it is now, is to imply that a paradigm will, inevitably, emerge. Does Mills' *Sociological Imagination* provide a basis for such a paradigm? If the majority of practitioners were converted to it, or cowed by it, would sociology race ahead with the speed of natural science?

I do not think so. Mills' work is not the stuff that paradigms are made of. His definition of the field is vast, his methodological suggestions are flexible and oriented to the individual, and above all, he insists implicitly and explicitly on the moral standard of social relevance. As Kuhn has pointed out, 'normal science', the kind of science that makes cumulative progress, cannot cope with such breadth and scope. It must examine finite and soluble puzzles in an established and conventional way. If it is confronted by external moral authorities and standards it will lose its way.[26] The reason

---

[22] See Kuhn, op. cit., p.109.
[23] ibid., pp.160 ff.
[24] Mills, 1960, op. cit., p.1.
[25] Kuhn, op. cit., pp.16, 47–48.
[26] ibid., p.168.

why scientists can put people on the moon and cannot solve the problems of war and poverty is that the first task involves finite, soluble problems within the ambit of normal science, whereas the latter problems are vast, complex and, within the terms of normal science, insoluble.

Mills tells us that the sociological imagination should concentrate on problems such as war and poverty. Within the social sciences the criterion for defining a topic as a problem that should be investigated must not be 'Can all the variables be measured?' or 'Is it clear, before we begin, that the problem is soluble?' But, 'Is the problem meaningful?' Will its investigation illuminate social issues and private troubles?

Conclusion

We cannot begin to understand society unless we take a macro view, a view that gives primacy to historical structures. This means that we must consider just those vast and complex questions that elude precise empirical measurement. The sociological imagination does not equip us with method and theory, it provides only a mood, a point of orientation. Its directions are not of a specific kind.

> The conclusion tells us what the essay was about, tying it together.

If we accept Kuhn's picture of natural science as just another curious form of human social activity, it is not necessarily to Mills' detriment that he has not set sociology on the road to cumulative progress. Any kind of dogma can make such progress if it acquires disciples and disposes of competition. Mills does not offer us dogma but a humanistic point of reference. If this is his fault, then much of the edifice of human culture fails with him.

But there is another danger that may have been less immediate for Mills when he was battling the orthodoxies of his day. While we must recognise the values that orient research, and we should, as moral agents, work if we can for the common good, we cannot do this if we allow values to dominate the outcome of the research process. It is one thing to acknowledge that values shape the direction of research, it is something else to allow them to affect its results.

We cannot separate values from the practice of social science, but we can and must distinguish between those values that define a field of inquiry, and which cannot by definition be avoided, and the bias that refuses to perceive unpalatable evidence. Research is conditioned, and advanced, by pre-existing ideas, but unless we allow these ideas to be 'disciplined by fact' the sociological imagination will once more betray its promise.

References

Arnold, M. (1970), *Literature and Dogma,* Ungar, New York.

Chamberlain, C. (1983), *Class Consciousness in Australia,* Allen and Unwin, Sydney.

Kuhn, T.S. (1970), *The Structure of Scientific Revolutions,* University of Chicago Press, Chicago.

Mills, C.W. (1960), 'Introduction', in C.W. Mills (Ed.), *Images of Man: The Classical Tradition in Sociological Thinking,* Braziller, New York.

Mills, C.W. (1970), *The Sociological Imagination,* Penguin, Harmondsworth.

Appendix 2

Sample research report

Subject: HASP303: Research Project
Semester 2: 2000
Swinburne University of Technology

Effects of Internet anonymity and disinhibition on self-disclosure
and identity change: an exploratory study

Name: Samantha Henderson
Tutor: Katharine Betts
Tutorial: Tuesday 11 a.m.
Room BA507

Introduction and Literature Review

The marriage of computers and communication has sparked a revolution of new ways of interacting. Undoubtedly, increased use of the Internet for many facets of life is going to impact dramatically on social interaction, relationships, education and work. Through the medium of the Internet, virtual communities have been created. These are communities that grow within the exchanges between people linked by communication networks. As Hearn et al. put it: 'These communities are not defined by race, colour or creed. They are borderless and occur without the factor of proximity' (1998: xvi). Rheingold says that they occur when a number of people have carried on a public discussion long enough, and with enough emotional engagement, for those involved to form a network of relationships in cyberspace (1994: 5).

Commonly, these online communities are found in such places as Internet Relay Chat (IRC) and MUDs (Multi User Domains, or Dungeons). Participants create a sense of community by recreating the non-verbal atmosphere that has been lost. They do this by 'using written words to describe how they *would* act and how the environment *would* appear in a shared mental model of a wholly constructed world' (Rheingold, 1994: 181). Thus cyberspace is showing us new ways of interacting, as well as new ways of exploring our own identities. Poster writes that people who observe and take part in online virtual communities agree that participants who engage in these communities intensely for long periods of time often experience a degree of fluidity in their personal identity (1994: 83–84).

With Internet communication, and in particular IRC and MUD facilities, it is possible for an individual to be anyone they want to be, of any sex or description. Vandore writes that: 'with the potential anonymity of an online presence, a paraplegic Anglo-Saxon male office worker can present himself as an athletic Jamaican female swimmer or vice-versa' (1995: 61). Some authors suggest that these changing notions of identity may appeal to us and that Computer-Mediated-Communication (CMC) media are dissolving the boundaries of identity (see Rheingold, 1994: 58). These media allow us to be anything, to experience everything as if it were real and to present ourselves to others in whatever way we like.

Because we feel more or less anonymous in various Internet locales, this may affect the way we act online. Wallace claims that research shows that anonymity online affects our behaviour and that one of these effects is disinhibition, or a decreased sense of the constraints on normal social behaviour (1999: 9). Anonymity allows people to escape certain bonds which, in normal interaction, shape their identity. Because of this people may behave differently on the Internet compared to real life. Wallace suggests that people can act in, 'very uninhibited ways when they think no-one can find out who they are. In the environments that offer this, people tend to let loose in both positive and negative ways' (1999: 239).

One of the more positive ways in which people 'let loose' is to disclose information about themselves that they would be reluctant to reveal to others in face-to-face interaction. Researchers have documented the disinhibiting effects of CMCs at some length, and self-disclosure is one of these effects. Rheingold argues that people reveal themselves in more intimate ways in cyberspace because of the anonymity created by computer screens and pseudonyms (1994: 27). Some researchers have even gone so far as to call the self-disclosing exchange between two people on CMCs *hyperpersonal*, a process which Wallace describes as sitting at a computer screen, feeling anonymous, distant and physically safe (1999: 151). This is often coupled with often feeling closer to those you are speaking to via CMC, than to people in the very next room:

> You may reveal more about yourself to them, feel more attraction to them, and express more emotions – even when all you have is a keyboard. At the keyboard you can concentrate only on yourself, your words, and the feelings you want to convey. You don't have to worry about how you look, or those extra pounds you meant to shed. ... [O]nline you can reallocate your energies to the message. (Wallace, 1999: 151)

In an online environment we can forget other cues that bombard us in real life (for example, good looks), and concentrate more on *what* it is we want to say. Reynolds et al. suggest that if a person is reluctant to talk about problems, emotional disclosure in a non-verbal environment is psychologically beneficial. In their study, they found that children found it easier to talk about emotionally disturbing events in writing, particularly when the person reading the piece was not known to them (Reynolds et al., 2000: 157–9). Their work shows that it is easier for people to disclose non-verbally and out of the immediate presence of others, circumstances which describe the Internet environment very well.

Some studies have focused on whether anonymity is associated with disinhibited behaviour, behaviour which is not inhibited by the social factors present in face-to-face communication. Sometimes the term *disinhibition* is interchangeable with *flaming*, the uninhibited expression of 'remarks containing swearing, insults, name calling and hostile comments' (Kiesler et al., 1984: 1127). But we should remember that flaming, or hostile behaviours are not the only indicators of disinhibition; emotions may also be expressed positively as can happen through self-disclosure. These differences between online and offline behaviour are most often explained by the fact that social cues are filtered out in online settings (Culnan & Markus, 1987: 431). Relational cues emerging from the physical context are missing, as are nonverbal cues, such as vocal qualities, bodily movement, facial expressions, and physical appearance (Parks & Floyd, 1996, [1]).

Heightened levels of self-disclosure have been found in many studies of Internet relationships. (See for example, Parks & Floyd, 1996, and Joinson, 1998.) Wilkins interviewed members of an online community of church workers, who all showed a relatively larger degree of disclosure online than in real life. One person commented: 'I know some of these people better than some of my oldest and best friends' (1991: 56). Parks and Floyd distributed surveys to various newsgroup users, 60 per cent of whom had formed personal relationships with other members of the group. Parks and Floyd asked participants about their online friendships and found that they generally agreed with such statements as: 'I usually tell this person how I feel'. The statement they most strongly disagreed with was: 'I would never tell this person anything intimate or personal about myself'. A study by Joinson found participants were less socially anxious and had higher self-esteem and a higher rate of self-disclosure online (1998). Joinson concluded that 'self-disclosure may be higher in CMC than [face-to-face] interactions' (1998: 47). He also identified some empirical theories as to why people are likely to feel disinhibited on the Internet. Theories of causes of Internet disinhibition include *deindividuation*, variations of which reduce both internal awareness and awareness of the public component of one's behaviour. Anonymity is the key to this deindividuation, and may play a role in a CMC users focusing on the task at hand rather than the recipient of their message or their own internal standards (Joinson, 1998: 49).

Other theories about self-disclosure online focus on social presence theory where researchers think that CMCs have a lower sense of social presence than in face-to-face meetings and that this promotes disclosure. Other theories again argue that the raising of private self-awareness whilst involved in CMCs might be linked with a decrease in concern for self-evaluation of behaviour (see Matheson & Zanna, cited in Joinson, 1998: 51). Social identity theorists equate anonymity with a lack of focus on oneself whilst in a social situation. They argue that this leads to the activation of social identities rather than personal ones, and go on to suggest that self-disclosure on CMCs may be dependent on the context (see Joinson, 1998: 53). Ultimately, though, underlying all these theories is the notion that when they are online people are able to concentrate more on what it is that they want to say, rather than the reception that they might get from others.

Paradoxically, online self-disclosure may go hand in hand with shifting identities. Because of relative anonymity Internet users often adopt different identities. Of course, we do not really become someone else when we do this online; what we are actually doing is splitting our identities into real-life and online parts. Online, we put a different face forward. We invent an online persona for ourselves. This persona may differ from our usual self only insofar as it can access vast amounts of information and resources quickly. Or the online persona may be a self we use to communicate socially, in which case it can take on personality traits unlike those we display in real life. It is common for many people to take on a novel online persona. This shows how different many of us feel when we communicate in cyberspace — a medium which seems to erase our physical bodies.

Sherry Turkle has studied this fluidity of identity extensively and reported it in *Life on the Screen: Identity in the Age of the Internet*, a book based largely on postmodern views of identity. Turkle focused on the way people interact in MUDs or role-playing games on the Internet, in which they play fictional characters in equally fictitious 'worlds', created with words. These 'worlds' exist in the windows that box off areas of our computer screens. We can only direct our attention to one window at a time but, in a sense, we are present in all of them simultaneously. Turkle concludes that these experiences can help people discover a postmodern way of knowing. Just as they recognise that the computer screen is merely a play of surface simulations to be explored, so do they come to see reality in the same way. She writes: 'If there is no underlying meaning, or a meaning we shall never know, postmodern theorists argue that the privileged way of knowing can only be through an exploration of surfaces' (1995: 13).

In her view everything is perceived as surfaces to be explored, with none of these surfaces having any more legitimacy than another. It follows from this that the embodied real life we live has no more basis in reality than Internet role playing games, or different identities in MUDs on IRC. If Turkle is right, users of these programs should discover that the notion of the unified self is a myth. Through playing different characters in different situations, they realise that none of these aspects of themselves is any less real than any other. Instead, reality becomes what is referred to as RL (Real Life), which for them is just another role-playing game. 'MUD players can develop a way of thinking in which life is made up of many windows and RL is only one of them' (Turkle, 1995: 192). MUDs provide opportunities to explore different types of identity. They may also allow them to express opinions freely and to become disinhibited.

For these people, participation in online chat networks can be a positive, life changing experience. They can choose whether or not to disclose their disability (if they have one) and they also have the advantage of anonymity. If someone has a low-self image because of their physical appearance or is extremely shy, these difficulties become almost non-issues online. Others cannot see what they look like, nor can they see the embarrassment of someone who is extremely shy. This is a unique new social situation and the lack of a synchronous face-to-face presence gives the actor much greater control over the developing definition of the situation. He or she has an opportunity to present an ideal self and to sustain that presentation throughout the interaction. They can practise talking to others, portraying themselves with more confidence than they might actually have in a face-to-face situation. This can be a system of positive re-inforcement of social behaviour, learned in an online environment, which they can then carry out into their real lives. Turkle tells the story of Gordon, who describes himself in junior high school as 'unpopular, overweight and unattractive' and who uses MUDs to explore a variety of flexible ways of presenting himself that can be used to negotiate challenges in the real world. 'For Gordon, playing on MUDs enabled a continual process of creation and recreation. The game has heightened his sense of self as a work in progress. He talks about his real self starting to pick up bits and pieces of his characters' (Turkle, 1995: 190).

Turkle argues that, with the new, postmodern, self: we don't have to rank or judge the various elements of the selves we develop, and we don't have to exclude any comments of these selves that seem incongruous or inconsistent (1995: 261). Once this liberation is accomplished, the self is prepared to play out all its fantasies, living life as a play of fictions. In effect, Turkle is describing how someone becomes an enthusiastic participant in the symbolic arenas of contemporary culture. People can then indulge their fantasies without guilt or discomfort. Nor is any of it a form of transgression, since the judging self that might label some fantasies off limits has been conveniently eliminated. We can then live like Stewart, who, Turkle tells us, is 'logged on to one MUD or another for at least forty hours a week'. She says: 'It seems misleading to call what he does there playing. He spends his time constructing a life that is more expansive than the one he lives in physical reality' (1995: 193).

The idea that we can create any sort of character we like online echoes the thoughts of Erving Goffman. In *The Presentation of Self in Everyday Life*, Goffman outlines a theory in which he believes life is like a play in which we are socialised to follow certain scripts. Thus, in every situation involving communication with others, we all assume roles and the various settings that we find ourselves in are a stage where we act out these roles. There is also an audience. For Goffman social interaction is a performance. The study of social life from this perspective is referred to as dramaturgy (Goffman, 1959: 17–76). Goffman reasons that 'dramaturgical plays' are handed down to us from myths and nursery rhymes and that they will vary between culture, gender, and other aspects of social location. We can analyse or explore the 'plays' or 'scripts' by observation and frame analysis. When we look at a transcript of what was said during a social interaction, coupled with descriptions of behaviours or non-verbal communication, it is like looking at the script of a play, act by act. This perspective can easily be applied to communication in an online environment.

Goffman's dramaturgy provides a framework for understanding the social interaction in online chat. He argues that the performances (which all have an audience) result in people being sensitive to how they are seen by others. Because of this we use *impression management* to try to compel others to react to us in the way that we wish (Goffman 1959: 1–15). For example, a man who wears a suit and tie at work and then changes to jeans and a shirt when watching the football with his friends is trying to give different groups of people an *impression* about himself. Goffman argues that when a discrepancy arises between the impressions that people try to give, and the actual impressions audiences receive, there is much embarrassment for the individual (1959: 13–14). This could provide a reason for why individuals might disclose more about themselves online; there is very little chance of being found out.

Statement of Objectives

Previous research suggests that there is a relationship between Internet anonymity, disinhibition, self-disclosure and identity exploring. The current study aims to help clarify this relationship. Turkle's postmodern ideas will form the basis of a discussion about identity, and exploration of this. Previous research has focused largely on her work in an attempt to *understand what* is happening with online communication, and the current study also aims to extend upon this by using the theory of dramaturgy in an attempt to *explain why* it is happening. The research question to be explored is this: What is the relationship between being anonymous online and disinhibition, self-disclosure and exploring different identities?

The key concepts include: Internet anonymity, Internet disinhibition, self-disclosure, willingness to self-disclose, and changing identity. I have nominally defined *Internet anonymity* as the degree to which Internet users can choose to remain anonymous. This is a rather ambiguous concept, because the amount of anonymity can vary greatly, depending on where you are on the net and what you are doing. In replying to an email from a friend a person could use their friend's name and their own name freely. (In some cases no choice is given because an email address clearly identifies the user. For example, johnsmith@swinburne.edu.au, is easily identifiable as John Smith who works for Swinburne University.) Yet in other environments, for example MUDs, it is easy for individuals to conceal their identity. Operationally, *anonymity* is defined as the incidence of, and the users' perception of, how anonymous they are on the Internet. *Internet disinhibition* is nominally defined as behaviour that on the Internet is 'less inhibited than comparative behaviour in real life…behaviour that is characterised by *apparent* reduction in concerns for self-presentation and judgement of others' (Joinson, 1998: 44). Although disinhibition encompasses behaviours ranging from flaming, or being impolite, to the use of capitals and exclamation marks, for the purposes of the current study it will be operationalised as expressing personal feelings towards someone else online (see Kiesler et al. cited in Joinson, 1998: 44).

Self-disclosure is nominally defined as the sharing of intimate information about oneself or one's feelings with another person (see

Taylor et al., 1997: 472). It is operationalised as the incidence of any such conversation with another person in a chat room. *Willingness to self-disclose* is nominally defined as how willing someone is to divulge intimate information about themselves, and operationalised for this study as how willing an individual says they might be to voluntarily indulge in a conversation in a chat room which contains self-disclosing content. The final concept of *identity change* is nominally defined as a change in basic personality (which may be pretended or experienced as genuine). It is operationally defined as changes of this kind which occur when a person is online, or characteristics of a person that emerge only when in an online environment. The definition includes *characteristics* that might emerge, because online identity exists on a continuum. On one end, there are those who completely rebuild themselves online (such as going from Stewart the geek in real life to Achilles the warrior on a MUD [Turkle 1995: 192–197]). On the other end, there are those who feel they are different only insofar as new, or stronger characteristics of their everyday selves emerge online. For example, someone might find it hard to be assertive in real life and be more assertive online, but they might not change their basic sense of who they are.

Method
Participants
There were twelve participants in the study (seven males and five females). Their ages ranged from 18 to 32, with the mean age being 23.1. Participants were purposively selected on the condition that they spent at least 15 hours a week online, and that this was for more than study or work purposes. Hours a week spent online by participants ranged from 15 to 60 (with a mean of 23.7 hours). Some of the participants were known to me as online friends or acquaintances. Acquaintances of these known participants were then used to recruit further participants.

Procedure
I sought informed consent from the participants and assumed that this had been granted when they agreed to participate. (Signed consent forms were impractical online.) Participants were interviewed with a semi-structured format in an online private chat. I decided that this was the most beneficial way of collecting data. Other researchers have noted that interviewing people online may have some disadvantages, such as not being able to identify the demographics of the population, and sometimes misinterpreting the context of typed answers (see Hamman, 1997 [1]). However, there are also clear benefits. Hamman notes that interviewing online gives cyberspace researchers the opportunity to observe participants in their own environment (1997 [6]). 'Interviewing [respondents] on their own territory... is the best strategy. It allows them to relax much more than they would in less familiar surroundings'

(Hammersley & Atkinson quoted in Hamman, 1995: 150). Research online is largely based on qualitative methods to examine the way in which meaning is constructed in online environments, and relies on analytical techniques developed for the analysis of conversations (see Cavanagh, 1999 [1]).

The interviews lasted for approximately an hour and a half and covered such themes as anonymity, its role in disinhibition, and if either of these affected the participant. For example, one question was: 'Do you feel that you cannot be traced?' (For a full copy of the questions used, see Appendix A.) Participants were also asked about their online identities and if these were the same or different to their sense of who they are in real life. The question of whether they had experimented with identities drastically different from their real-life selves or with multiple selves was also discussed at length. For example, participants were asked: 'Has your identity online ever been drastically different to who you feel you are in real life?' Issues of self-disclosure were raised. Points of interest were the *amount* of disclosure online, as well as the *types* of disclosure. Was it qualitatively the same or different to disclosure in real life? For example, participants were asked: 'Think about how much you self-disclose in real life. Is this less, more, or the same to the amount that you might disclose about yourself online?' After the interviews, transcripts of the chat were copied and pasted for storage as a file, with pseudonyms assigned to each participant to ensure confidentiality. The transcripts were then analysed for themes relevant to the research question.

Results

The first issue explored with participants was anonymity, to determine whether participants felt anonymous online or not, and whether this was a factor in their online behaviour. Generally participants felt that they were largely anonymous, mostly because the average person online did not have the skills to trace them. Participants also held the view that, because the Internet is so large scale, many people had no *interest* in finding out exactly who they were. Long-time Internet user, Ben, demonstrated this by saying: 'I feel as anonymous as I like to be. I know that I can be traced, and I know how to do it, but why people would bother is another issue.' These thoughts were echoed by Herc, 21, who said: 'The people I talk to probably can't trace me, unless they are a hacker, and likely wouldn't want to trace me anyway'. Only two of the 12 participants said that they did not feel anonymous online, and these two felt that this was not an issue because they didn't do anything online that they were embarrassed about.

Whilst discussing issues of multiple online identities, participants were presented with a statement (taken from Turkle), that read: 'The Internet has contributed to thinking about identity as a multiplicity. On it, people are able to build a self by cycling through many selves. Online, people can develop a way of thinking in which life is made up of many windows and real life is only one of them' (Turkle, 1995: 12). They were then asked to comment on the statement, and perhaps agree or disagree.

Most participants did agree with the statement in general, although many disagreed with the final premise of the quote, believing instead that real life *was* more important than online identities. It was not just another window. They commonly thought that, although online selves are important, real-life selves were much more meaningful. When asked which she gave more weight to, Stella, 20, said:

> There have been a lot of times when I have given more to my online self and [my] real life self has just gone astray. It depends how much time I spend on the net. If I spend more time on the net than socializing in real life then the net gets first priority and becomes more important to me. Real life self is definitely more important though, because it is where you have to make your contacts for life and make friends and get a job. It's fun making friends on the net, but really if you don't have a good life personality you won't get by. What's the point of having heaps of people who adore you on the net and no one in real life who does? The net people can't do anything to help you survive in [the] real world.

Doug agreed, saying: 'Real life is the only life. There are no "windows". There is your real life and you choose to act the way you want. I think online is more of a fantasy than a window to oneself.' Most participants agreed with Doug's sentiments. One said that cycling through identities online is exactly what people do in real life anyway. Nigel, 25, believed that we all present different characters in real life in different situations, and that doing this online is no great discontinuity. He said: 'In real life people also [cycle through identities], but we don't see it occur as much because of the same reason it works so well online ... anonymity.'

Most participants said that they felt that it was individuals who were new to the Internet ('newbies') who tended to explore their identities online. Seven of the participants had greatly experimented online; all of the seven had become members of the opposite sex at least once, to 'see what it was like,' and perhaps, to 'get a kick.' Others had experimented to some degree, but felt that their online selves were not very different to who they were in real life. Stella said:

> It's all a reaction to who you are chatting to. I have gone through stages of being a different personality—sometimes a happy and positive person, sometimes an empathising, caring one. I guess I have never been anyone that would not fit into my morals as a real life person though.

Of the seven participants who had changed their identities online, most only experimented once, and only one still experimented regularly, despite being a long-time Internet user. Most participants said that when they had been online a while and had had their turn at experimenting, they went back to being who they felt they were in real life.

Doug said: 'Pretending gets boring when you do it all the time…and it's hard to keep track of'. The participants commonly felt that the Internet was a good place to explore aspects of the self, and most condoned it. However if it was the participant themselves who had been tricked then such exploration wasn't as freeing as they had first thought. Suddenly issues of trust were involved. For these individuals, playing with identity online was all well and good for them, but when it happened *to* them, it was seen as devious and a complete breach of trust. Participants who felt that they had never lied about themselves online were more likely to feel betrayed by someone who revealed him or herself as something different. For these people, it is the online honesty that makes the interactions important and meaningful.

Mitch, 22, recalled a time that he thought he was talking to a female online, and the person revealed themselves to be really male. He said: 'That was the end of us chatting. The fact that they were male didn't bother me, just the fact that we had chatted for a while, and *then* the truth arose. I didn't want to chat to a liar.' Interestingly, Mitch also freely admitted to doing the same thing to others online as a newbie. When he first started using the Internet to chat, he said: '[I] became obsessed with trying to impress people on the net, although I quickly realised there was no use. If people don't like you for what you are they are not worth chatting to.'

I asked participants whether they felt their behaviour was any less inhibited online, and they almost unanimously agreed, with typical comments being, 'you can't get punched in the face for calling someone a moron online.' Another person said, 'I may freely argue with someone who is being a jerk online, whereas in real life I'd probably keep my mouth shut to keep my teeth.' The same person also said:

> I'm a fairly anti-social person in real life. I'm always too self conscious and generally I keep to myself a lot, probably just because I'm worried people will find me weird and then I won't know what to say to them. I'm not a total outcast or anything but the Internet definitely makes it easier to express my opinion.

Eight participants suggested, without prompting, that a way in which they were less inhibited online was to self-disclose more. They felt less inhibited in the ways in which they spoke to people as well as in the amount of information that they disclosed, as well as in the types of information that they disclosed. One person said:

> I feel very comfortable talking to people on the Internet, much more so than in person most of the time. You don't

have to worry about fitting in as much and if someone isn't compatible with you, then you can just ignore them and close the window. In person you have to still try and make conversation and be polite... It's too much hassle sometimes.

After I specifically asked them about self-disclosure, all but one participant admitted that they did find it much easier to talk about embarrassing topics online, even compared with talking to their best friends. Connie, 24, described how she often chose to disclose things of a personal nature to her friends over the Internet, despite having been best friends with other people in the 'real' world for over ten years. She said: 'Even though online environments seem very real, there is also something removed about it. I suppose it's the lack of cues that makes it easier to talk to friends about embarrassing things online'.

In discussing online relationships with people, participants felt generally that they were qualitatively different to relationships in real life, but not more or less significant. Chloe, 21, who worked with computers and was online up to 60 hours a week said: 'Online and real life friends are very different. There are things that only online friends know about me, things I can't talk about with real life friends because they may be involved'. However, she also pointed that there are a lot of times that she would ask her real-life friends for advice and would self-disclose, and that there are 'little things that I do, part of who I am, those fundamental things that my real life friends know so well and my online friends will never see'. By this she meant the way she bites her nails, the dimple that appears when she smiles, and other idiosyncrasies.

Although many participants shared Chloe's view that real life friends were good for advice, they also noted that they felt better getting advice from their online friends, because online friends could be more objective as they were slightly removed from the situation. Types of information divulged to people online differed in that very embarrassing subjects were talked about online, as well as problems with real-life friends.

Discussion

The results indicate that a relationship is present between Internet anonymity, disinhibition, self-disclosure and changing identities. Furthermore that relationship is a complex one, centring around the concept of anonymity. Participants generally agreed that they felt anonymous enough for this to play a role both in the information they disclosed to others online, as well as in the identities they assumed. Most participants identified anonymity as the key reason why they felt able to become less inhibited, to self-disclose more, and perhaps even to change their identity.

In regards to changing their identity, just over half of the people interviewed had done this at some stage. The findings here were somewhat mixed, but generally the results of previous research have been replicated, but with some major differences. Turkle (1995: 263) argues that when individuals become used to navigating the Internet and become accustomed to how things operate, they form a sense of comfort and thus feel free to explore identities. However, the current study indicated that it was the newbies who tended to explore their identity. Reece, 18, suggested that this was because: 'The newbies love the chance to revel in their anonymity. It's new and exciting when you first start [chatting]…you can do *anything* and no-one can find out who you are.' (Reece chats on the Internet for 40 hours a week.) Dave, 32, echoed these statements, remarking that the people on the Internet are real people, and eventually they almost 'calm down' and return to being themselves after a period of time online:

> It's all the newbies who experiment. People like myself who have been in cyberspace a long time are, in a sense, *over* pretending to be someone drastically different. Sure, we all might be a bit different online, a little more assertive here, a bit flirtier there, but after you've had your initial fun, pretending loses it's [sic] spark. That's when you get to the stage of building *trust* with people online, which is definitely the key to online relationships.

Many of the participants felt that trust was important. This is indicated by the interesting finding that individuals felt that it was okay for them to explore a different identity online, but that when other people did it to them, they felt betrayed. In a few cases, such an experience was enough for the individual to make the decision not to differ too drastically from their real life identity at all.

To understand the importance of other selves in cyberspace, we need to step back a bit and consider what exactly we mean by 'in real life' and the self who exists there. Obviously, the phrase 'in real life' refers to how we appear physically, since you cannot literally be seen online. But it also indicates something about who you are in person – a set of behaviours which cannot be seen even in pictures – the way you express yourself verbally, your hand gestures, a certain demeanour. This was indicated by Chloe's ideas, discussed earlier, that online friends cannot see 'little things that I do, part of who I am, those fundamental things that my real life friends know so well.' Most importantly, perhaps, existing 'in real life' means dealing directly with the material world. This may mean the sheer, physical fact of our racial, gendered, and sexual bodies and how other people react to them without bothering to learn about who we are as individuals.

Considered in this light, it seems that our online personas are just one more series of selves that our everyday lives require us to create in order to deal with a variety of situations. The difference between a cyberspace persona and a real life persona is that the cyberspace persona is one more step removed from material reality. Unlike a real life persona, the cyberspace persona does not exist in a direct relationship to survival on any level. It is a surplus personality, a self we take on for pleasure or just because it seems right. There is no longer just one 'real-life' self; we have a series of selves we put on. The exact purpose of these selves is unknown. However, they do seem to play a role in an exploratory fashion, allowing individuals to find aspects of themselves not often displayed in real life. Given time and practice, these individuals are able to apply the social skills they learn online to a real life situation. Some participants felt that this was indeed the case. Kelly summed up general feelings perfectly with her statement that:

> In real life, I'm quite shy and don't express my opinion very much, something that is easier for me to do online. Because of this, I'm finding that people online *like* talking to me, and I *do* have some interesting opinions. These realisations have been spilling over into real life lately, and I've become much more outgoing because of my Internet experiences.

Having Internet experiences spilling over into real life indicates how, for many intense users of the Internet, it is becoming a very pervasive part of their lives. Not only is the Internet spilling over into real life, but real life is becoming part of the Internet. This is evident in Nigel's point that people also 'cycle through' identities in real life. By this he is suggesting that there are different personalities we have for different audiences. This fits well with Goffman's impression management whereby individuals put forth different personas in order to get desired reactions from others. Internet users only have a keyboard with which to present impressions that they might want to make. But as Goffman argues, motivation is the key (1959: 32–33).

According to Wallace, you might want to be liked by your audience, you might want to dominate them, to throw yourself on their mercy or to have them fear or respect you (1999: 28). We choose tactics for our self-presentation that we hope will accomplish our goal. Nigel said: '[Online] I have friends I can talk to, friends I can make jokes with, friends I can talk sexually with, but not all of them fit into all the categories. Some people don't need to hear about my fears or pains or desires and others may not want to know why the chicken crossed the road.' Nigel's words suggest that his experiences are a result of wanting to give different impressions to different people, and that impression management exists even in cyberspace.

That we feel able, or compelled, to change ourselves in order to enter cyberspace is not due to the nature of cyberspace itself. Rather, it is an extension of the way our real-life society operates. In everyday life, people are encouraged to split themselves: with different personalities, they can function more effectively at work, and then return home to play, to the family, to a club, and so on. We are used to thinking of different social environments, like cyberspace, as requiring us to be different people. In fact, one might argue that MUD and IRC identities are versions of the masks we wear in any work or public situation. Online, we are more aware (and perhaps more in control) of the masks we put on in order to meet people, but a swordplay on a MUD can be just as real as a CEO's arrogant bluster at a meeting.

The notion of having these many selves as masks resonates with Goffman's theory of dramaturgy. Goffman also argues that when a discrepancy arises between the impressions we want to give and those we actually give, it can result in embarrassment (1959: 12). The anonymity of being online removes the possibility of being caught out trying to be someone else, or self-disclosing private information. Consequently individuals might be more likely to engage in these sorts of behaviour online. Those participants who indulged in such behaviours indicated that it was a result of anonymity, and that they wouldn't do so if they weren't anonymous. This suggests the relationship between anonymity, disinhibition and changing identities is complex. The current study suggests, however, that because of feeling anonymous, individuals become less inhibited about their behaviour online, and feel free to change their identities.

The results also indicate that because individuals are anonymous and less inhibited, they may tend to self-disclose more online. Mitch said: 'People tend to express their emotions more on the net. In real life especially, with just friends, people don't express their feelings or worries to each other, whereas the net takes away some sort of embarrassment or discomfort.' Although around half of participants felt that they disclosed more online, there were those who did not feel that self-disclosing online was any different to real life. Ben said: 'I know that I may not be found out, but I'm not going to let just anybody in … it's no different to real life, some people you like, some you don't'. Herc too, talked about issues of knowing the person online well before disclosing to them. He admitted that this might be problematic however.

> If you get attached to someone online then it can be almost as hard to disclose certain things to them as if they were in person. Sure there isn't the pain of them laughing in your face, but it can still be hard if you care enough that you don't want their perception of you to change or for what you say to make things awkward between you.

Not surprisingly, the individuals who didn't self-disclose online any more than in real life were also generally the same people that did not change their identity online. They, in some cases, felt less inhibited, but that this wasn't a drastic variation on their real self. Ben said: 'It's the same me, but less inhibited, I don't paint myself any differently than in real life.' These users were the ones for whom trust was important. Building relationships online to them was about having trust and respect for other people by not changing basic details about themselves, and expecting the same in return. These participants indicated that they would be very hurt if they found out that they were being lied to online, and Wallace warns about 'being perceived as a manipulative social chameleon who fakes an impression for social [or any] gain' (1999: 29). She relates this to Goffman's impression management, saying that we work very hard to manage the impressions we present but we don't want others to know how hard we work.

Joinson (1998: 44) highlights theories associated with disinhibition centring around the idea that the individual is able to concentrate more on what it is that they want to say, rather than the reception their words might get from others. These notions weren't tested at length, but it can be seen from issues arising from the interviews that lack of social cues is a factor in being disinhibited, and perhaps in disclosing more. As we have seen, Connie said: 'I suppose it's the lack of cues that makes it easier to talk to friends about embarrassing things online.'

This research has been preliminary and exploratory, but the answers to the research question seem clear. Anonymity online does encourage disinhibition and self disclosure. It also encourages the trying out of different identities. While for some the different identities they present online are only a marginal refocus of aspects of their real-life selves, for others there can be a period of extensive exploration of new personas. Further research is needed to explore the reasons for the association between anonymity and these phenomena. However the data analysed so far give some credence to Goffman's dramaturgical perspective. In this perspective, while we play a variety of roles and try to manage the impression others have of us, we nonetheless believe that we do have a core real self. Turkle's postmodern notion that so-called real life is just another window and that face-to-face selves are not more real to us than virtual selves is not generally supported.

Apart from exploring reasons for the effects of anonymity on online behaviour, another area that may generate interesting further research is the finding that it tends to be the newbies who change their identity. The current study did not look at users who were particularly new to the Internet, or who only used it lightly. It might be beneficial to select a sample that included new users so as to ascertain whether this perception that Internet veterans have of them is correct.

This highlights a problem with the current study, in that the sample may have been biased due to sampling strategy. With a more systematic way of sampling Internet users, perhaps a stratified sample, with equal numbers of new users and old users, a clearer picture of the issues involved with being a newbie may emerge. Another problem with the present study is the medium on which the interviews were conducted. Interviewing online may have allowed participants to lie more easily about their answers. However, the study itself shows that people are more willing to disclose online, and thus would find it easier to be interviewed in the same manner. Also, because they were interviewed via computer, participants had a bit longer to sit and think about their answers, rather than having to answer straight away, as they might have in the immediate presence of an interviewer.

The most important finding is that, contrary to previous research, individuals seemed to change their identity more as new users than as veterans. Turkle (1995: 88–101, 186–234) interviewed participants in particular about their MUD experiences, an environment in which people are not meant to be themselves, and hardly could be when playing anything from a rabbit to an evil goblin. Chatting to friends met online is different and this may explain the different findings. Perhaps if I had asked some specific questions about MUDs, it would have been easier to tease out the issues involved in changing identity, and the seeming contradiction of Turkle's findings would have been resolved.

As human beings, we are always searching for ways to re-imagine ourselves and our relationships with each other. It is true that the ways people alter their identities on the net are not always Utopian or progressive. But sometimes, a new culture like that found in cyberspace gives us a taste of what the world would be like if we were to change what we are by becoming who we want to be. The Internet opens up important opportunities to meet people and share relationships with them that are just as special as those relationships we have in real life.

References

Cavanagh, A. (1999), 'Behaviour in public? Ethics in online ethnography', *Cybersociology Magazine* (6) [online], available at: <http://www.socio.demon. co.uk/magazine/6/cavanagh.html> (accessed 21/4/00, last modified: 6/8/99).

Culnan, M.J., & Markus, M.L. (1987), 'Information technologies', in F. Jablin, L.L Putnam, K. Roberts and L. Porter (Eds), *Handbook of Organizational Communication*, Sage, Newbury Park, CA.

Goffman, E. (1959), *The Presentation of Self in Everyday Life*, Doubleday: New York.

Hamman, R. (1997), 'The application of ethnographic methodology in the study of cybersex,' *Cybersociology Magazine*, no. 1 (no volume number) [online], available at: <http://www.socio.demon.co.uk/magazine/1/plummer.html> (accessed: 21/04/00, date last modified unavailable).

Hearn, G., Mandeville, T., & Anthony, D. (1998), *The Communication Superhighway: Social and Economic Change in the Digital Age*, Allen and Unwin, Sydney.

Joinson, A (1998), 'Causes and implications of disinhibited behaviour on the Internet', in J. Gackenbach (Ed.), *Psychology and the Internet: Intrapersonal, Interpersonal and Transpersonal Implications*, Academic Press, San Diego.

Kiesler, S., Siegel, J., & McGuire, T.W. (1984), 'Social psychological aspects of computer mediated communication', *American Psychologist*, vol. 39, no. 10, pp. 1123–1134.

Parks, M., & Floyd, K. (1996), 'Making friends in cyberspace,' *Journal of Computer-Mediated Communication*, vol. 1, no. 4 [online], available at: <http://jcmc. indiana.edu/vol1/issue4/vol1no4.html> (accessed: 21/04/00, date last modified unavailable).

Poster, M. (1994), 'A second media age?', *Arena Journal*, no. 3 (no volume number), pp. 49–91.

Reynolds, M., Brewin, C.R., & Saxton, M. (2000), 'Emotional disclosure in school children', *Journal of Child Psychology and Psychiatry*, vol. 41, no. 2, pp. 151–159.

Rheingold, H. (1994), *The Virtual Community: Surfing the Internet*, Minerva: London.

Taylor, S., Peplau, L., & Sears, D. (1997), *Social Psychology*, Prentice Hall: New Jersey.

Turkle, S. (1995), *Life on the Screen: Identity in the Age of the Internet*, Simon and Schuster: New York.

Vandore, S. (1995), 'When information wants to be free', *Australian Personal Computer*, February, pp. 60–63.

Wallace, P. (1999), *The Psychology of the Internet*, Cambridge University Press: Cambridge.

Wilkins, H. (1991), 'Computer talk: Long distance conversations by computer', *Written Communication*, vol. 8, no. 1, pp. 56–78.

Appendix: Questions and themes covered in semi-structured interviews

ANONYMITY

First, I need to ask some basic questions about your use of the Internet.
- How often do you use the Internet? (hrs/week)
- Do you use the Internet for more than just school or work purposes? (for example to socialise?)
- Do you think the Internet is a relatively anonymous means of communication?
- How anonymous do you feel on the Internet?
- Do you feel that you cannot be traced?
- Why or why not?

IDENTITY CHANGING

I'm going to give you a statement, and I want you to think about it and comment:

> 'The Internet has contributed to thinking about identity as a multiplicity. On it, people are able to build a self by cycling through many selves. Online, people can develop a way of thinking in which life is made up of many windows and real life is only one of them.'

- Do you feel that you have ever 'cycled through identities' on the net?
- Has your identity online been drastically different compared to who you feel you are in real life? For example, have you ever changed your sex?
- Why or why not?
- If not, or even if so…what do you think of people who do this?
- Is it fair of other people not to 'be themselves' online?

So we have reached some agreement then, that cyberspace is freeing. I have another statement I want you to think about:

> 'For all the talk about how freeing cyberspace is, I've found that you can't pry into people's personalities from their furiously typing fingers …' Do you think that when people *can* be what they want, there are still some parts of their inherent personality that show through?

- Do you agree with this?
- Why? Why not?

DISINHIBITION

Going back to the degree of anonymity you feel—

Research suggests that the degree of anonymity affects our behaviour in important ways and leads to disinhibition — a lowering of normal social constraints on behaviour.

Do you feel your behaviour is any less inhibited online? For example, is it easier for you to express your opinion, whether positive or negative?

Some commentators suggest that people can act in 'very uninhibited ways' when they think no-one can find out who they are. In the environments that offer this, people tend to let loose in both positive and negative ways.

- Do you agree with this?
- Why? Why not?

SELF-DISCLOSURE

- Do you feel comfortable chatting to people on the Internet? Is it easy for you to disclose personal information about yourself in say, a private chat?
- Why or Why not?
- Think of how much you self-disclose in real life. Is this more or less than the amount you might disclose about yourself online?
- Why do you think this might be?
- I am interested in whether you disclose more or less on the Internet, but also, I'd like to know if you feel that the information you may disclose to someone online may be different to information you disclose in real life?
- How is this information different? Do you feel less or more comfortable talking about more personal information in online conversations, as opposed to real life?
  Does this depend on certain circumstances? What are these?

NOTE: As this is a semi-structured interview, some additional questions were asked depending on the participants' answers. This means that not all of the interviews consisted of exactly the same questions.

Appendix 3

Glossary of grammatical terms

by Gavin Betts

The following list contains the grammatical terms of traditional English grammar. If you are not familiar with these start with the **parts of speech**, viz **adjective, adverb, article, conjunction, interjection, noun, preposition, pronoun, verb**. These are the categories into which words are classified for grammatical purposes.

Active see **Voice**.

Adjective An adjective is a word which qualifies (i.e. tells us of some quality of) a noun or pronoun: *a **high** building; a **short** giraffe; the politician was **intelligent**; she is **thin**.*

Adverb Adverbs qualify verbs, adjectives, or other adverbs: *she talks **quickly**; an **extremely** fat man; the ship was going **very slowly**.* Certain adverbs can qualify nouns and pronouns: ***even** a child can see that.* They may even qualify a whole clause: *we went to London last year; we **also** saw Paris.*

Apposition A noun (or noun phrase) is in apposition to another noun or pronoun when it follows by way of explanation and is exactly parallel in its relation to the rest of the sentence: *he, **a just man**, was wrongly convicted; I, **the undersigned**, will inform my solicitor.*

Article English has two articles ***the*** and ***a/an***. ***The*** is called the definite article because a noun preceded by it refers to someone or something definite: ***the** cat belonging to the neighbours kept me awake last night.* ***A/an*** is called the indefinite article because a noun preceded by it refers to someone or something indefinite: *No, I do not want **a** dog.*

Attributive *Attributive* and *predicative* are the terms applied to the two ways in which adjectives can be used. An adjective used attributively forms a phrase with the noun it qualifies, and in English always comes immediately before it: ***modern** America, a **tall** mountain, the **competent** doctor.* An adjective used predicatively tells us what is predicated of, or asserted about, a person or thing. A verb is always involved in this use, and in English a predicative adjective always, in prose, follows the noun or pronoun it qualifies, generally with the verb coming between them: *men are **mortal**, the accountant was **bald**.* This use frequently involves the verb *to be*, but there are other possibilities: *the shop-keeper was considered **honest**, we thought the tax agent **avaricious**.* All adjectives can be used in either way, with the exception of some possessive adjectives in English such as *my, mine* (the first can be only attributive, the second only predicative).

Auxiliary verb Many tenses in English are formed with the present or past participle of a verb together with some part of *have* or *be* (or both); when so used the latter are called auxiliary verbs: *he **was** running when I saw him*; *I **have** read this glossary five times*; *we **have been** working for the past week at Sociology*. These combinations (*was running, have read*, etc.) are called composite tenses. Other auxiliary verbs in English are *shall, will, should, would*. See also **Participle** and **Tense**.

Case In any type of expression where it occurs, a noun (or pronoun) stands in a certain relationship to the other words, and this relationship is determined by the meaning we want to convey. The two sentences *my brothers bite dogs* and *dogs bite my brothers* contain exactly the same words but have opposite meanings, which are shown by the relationship in each sentence of the nouns *brothers* and *dogs* to the verb *bite*; here (as is normal in English) this relationship is indicated by word order. In some languages it is indicated by the form a noun takes when used in a particular case. In English we still have this system with pronouns; we say *I saw her today*, we cannot say *me saw her today* because *I* is the nominative case, required here to show the subject of the verb, whereas *me* is the accusative case and is used as the object of a verb (*they saw me*) or after a preposition (*you must avoid running into me*). With nouns in English we only have one case which can be indicated by an ending and this is the genitive; *girl's, boy's*. See also **Pronoun** and **Subject**.

Clause A clause is a group of words forming a sense unit and containing one finite verb, e.g. *the farmer **feared** the travelling salesman*; *I **am** not happy today* (the finite verb is in bold type). There are two types of clauses: **main clauses**, which can stand on their own, and **subordinate clauses**, which cannot. In the sentence *The bookmaker owned a house which had cost much money*, the first five words constitute the main clause and this forms a complete sense unit; if, however, you were to say to a friend *which had cost much money* and nothing else, you would risk being thought odd because these words constitute a subordinate clause and do not form an independent sense unit. Subordinate clauses are divided into **adverbial** which function as adverbs, **adjectival**, which function as adjectives, and **noun** clauses, which function as nouns. See also **Finite**.

Comparison (of adjectives and adverbs) see **Inflexion**.

Composite tenses A composite tense is one that is formed with an auxiliary verb. See **Auxiliary Verb**.

Conjunction Conjunctions are **joining words**. Some conjunctions can join clauses, phrases or individual words (e.g. *and, or*) but most have a more restricted use. Those that are used to join clauses are divided into **co-ordinating** conjunctions (*and, or, but*), which join a main clause to a preceding one (*I went to the supermarket, but you were not there*), and **subordinating** conjunctions, which subordinate one clause to another (*the doctor came because I was ill*).

Finite This term is applied to those forms of verbs which can function by themselves as the verbal element of a clause. The only non-finite forms of a verb in English are participles and infinitives. We can say *our football team defeated their opponents* because *defeated* is a finite form of the verb *to defeat*. We cannot say *our football team to have defeated their opponents* because *to have defeated* is an infinitive and therefore non-finite, nor can we say (as a full sentence) *our football team having defeated their opponents* because *having defeated* is a participle. See also **Clause**.

Gender In English we only observe natural gender (apart from such eccentricities as supposing ships feminine). If we are talking about a man we refer to him by the masculine pronoun *he*, but we refer to a woman by the feminine pronoun *she*, and we refer to a thing, such as a table or chair, by the neuter pronoun *it*.

Imperative see **Mood**.

Indicative see **Mood**.

Infinitive Infinitives are those parts of a verb which in English are normally preceded by *to*, e.g. *to see, to be seen, to have seen, to have been seen*. These are, respectively, the present active, present passive, past active, and past passive, infinitives of the verb *see*. See also **Tense**.

Interjection Interjections are words used to express one's emotions. They do not form part of sentences. Examples are *wow! alas!*

Intransitive This is a term applied to verbs which cannot, because of their meaning, take a normal object, e.g. *come, die, go*. The opposite term is **transitive**; transitive verbs (e.g. *make, hit, repair*) can take an object. *He hit the man* is a perfectly possible sentence, but *he dies the man* is nonsense. Sometimes in English we have pairs of verbs, one transitive and the other intransitive, which are obviously connected in sense and etymology, as *to fall* and *to fell*. We can say *John is falling from the tree* but *John is falling the tree* is without sense. If we mean *John is causing the tree to fall*, we can say *John is felling the tree*; hence *to fall* is intransitive, *to fell* is transitive.

Mood is a term applied to verbs.

> **Imperative** is the mood used to give an order: **do** *this immediately!*
>
> **Indicative** is the mood used to express a fact: *the doctor* **operated** *on me yesterday.*
>
> **Subjunctive** In other languages the subjunctive mood expresses what the speaker wills, expects, desires or considers possible. Only a few relics of the subjunctive survive in English (*if I* **were** *you;* **be** *that as it may, i.e. let that* **be** *as it may; long* **live** *the Queen!*). In modern English the functions once performed by the subjunctive mood have been taken by auxiliary verbs, e.g. **let** *that man go!; I* **would** *not* **do** *that for all the tea in China;* **may** *that not* **happen!**

Noun A noun is a naming word: **book, river, truth, Paul, Melbourne.** Proper nouns are those we write with a capital letter, all others are common nouns.

Number A noun, or pronoun, or verb is normally either **singular** or **plural**.

Object A noun or pronoun which is the object of an active verb suffers or receives the action of that verb: *the student wrote an* **essay**; *the free offer tempted many* **customers**; *the tourists lost their* **luggage**. By definition we cannot have an object of this sort after intransitive verbs or (normally) after verbs in the passive voice. It is sometimes called a **direct object** to distinguish it from an **indirect object** which we get after verbs of saying and giving: *he* *told a story to **the child***. In English we can express this slightly differently: *he told **the child** a story*; but *child* is still the indirect object because the direct object is *story*. See also **Case**.

Participle Participles are those forms of a verb which function as adjectives: *the **running** horse, a **fallen** tree*. Some participles are formed with one or more auxiliary verbs, e.g. ***having fallen** on the road, the unfortunate man was run over by a tram*; ***having been attacked** by five dogs on my way home I decided to catch a taxi*. Participles may consist of one word (e.g. *fallen*) or more than one (e.g. *having been attacked*). They are also used to form composite tenses; see **Auxiliary verb** and **Tense**.

Passive see **Voice**.

Person There are three persons, **first**, **second** and **third**. **First person** is the person(s) speaking, i.e. *I* or *we*; **second person** is the person(s) spoken to, i.e. *you*; and **third person** is the person(s) or thing(s) spoken about, i.e. *he, she, it, they*. The term **person** has reference to pronouns and also to verbs because finite verbs must agree with their subject in **number** and **person**. Naturally, when we have a noun as subject of a verb, e.g. *the dog is running across the road*, the verb is in the third person.

Phrase A phrase is an intelligible group of words which does not have a finite verb: *into the woods, the dealer's five used cars*. A phrase can only be used by itself in certain circumstances, as in an answer to a question.

Predicate The predicate is what is said about the subject of a clause. In *Marx wrote this book* the subject is *Marx* and what is said about him (*wrote this book*) is the predicate. In *the civil servant was furious* the adjective *furious* is used predicatively because it is part of the predicate (*was furious*).

Predicative see **Attributive**.

Preposition Prepositions are words which govern a noun or pronoun and show the relationship of the noun or pronoun to the rest of the sentence: *my cousin went **to** Sydney; we live **in** Adelaide; I saw John **with** him*.

Pronoun Pronouns stand in place of nouns. The English personal pronouns are: *I, you, he, she, it, we, they* (in the accusative case *me, you, him, her, it, us, them*). Other words such as *this, that* can function as pronouns (***this** is nonsense, I do not like **that***) or as adjectives (*I do not like **that** habit*); for convenience they are called demonstrative pronouns. We also have reflexive pronouns (*he loves **himself***) and relative pronouns (*I do not like the woman **who** was here*). See also **Case**.

Sentence A sentence is a unit of speech which normally contains at least one main clause. It may be either a statement, question or command. See also **Clause** and **Finite**.

Subject A noun or pronoun which is the subject of an active verb performs the action of that verb: *the **lecturer** went on a journey to Alice Springs; the **estate agent** amassed a large amount of money; on the third day the **patient** died*. It is normal to speak of the subject as governing its verb. In English a finite verb's person and number are determined by the subject. We cannot say *I is* because *I* is the first person singular pronoun and *is* is the third person singular of the verb *to be* (present tense); we must here use the first person (singular) form *am*. Likewise we must say *we are* and not *we am* because *we* is plural. An easy way to find the subject in English is to put *who* or *what* in front of the verb; with the sentence *the ship was hit by a submerged rock*, we ask the question *what was hit by a submerged rock?* and the answer, *the ship*, is the subject of the clause. See also **Case** and **Voice**.

Subjunctive see **Mood.**

Tense Tense is a term applied to verbs. Every finite form of a verb, as well as participles and infinitives, indicates that the action or state expressed takes place in a particular time. The verb in *I am sick* refers to the present, in *I will be* sick to the future. These temporal states are called tenses, and these fall into three categories: **present, future, past**. Within these categories we have the following tenses (**note that many tenses in English are formed with a participle and either one or two auxiliary verbs**):

Present

> **Present simple** (*I **knit** regularly*)
> **Present continuous** (*I **am knitting** five socks*)
> **Present perfect** (*I **have knitted** ten jumpers*)

Future

> **Future simple** (*I **shall/will knit** you a vest*)
> **Future continuous** (*When you call tomorrow I **shall/will** probably **be knitting***)
> **Future perfect** (*By the end of this week I **shall/will have knitted** six jumpers*)

Past

> **Past simple** (*I **knitted** an interesting bootie yesterday*)
> **Past continuous** (*I **was knitting** when the refrigerator exploded*)
> **Past perfect (or pluperfect)** (*When the cat strangled itself in my wool I decided I **had knitted** enough*)

The tenses of English verbs often consist of more than one word because they are formed using auxiliaries and participles, as in the present perfect, *I have knitted.*

Transitive see **Intransitive.**

Verb A verb, when finite, is the **doing** or **being** word of its clause. It must agree with the subject in **person** and **number**. For non-finite forms of verbs see **finite**. A finite verb varies according to **person**, **number**, **tense**, **mood**, and **voice**.

Voice is a term applied to verbs, whether finite or non-finite. In English there are two voices, **active** and **passive**. The subject of an active verb is the doer of the action; *the soldier **lifted** his rifle*, and if the verb is transitive it usually has an object (in this case *his rifle*). With a passive verb the subject suffers or receives the action: *the rifle **was lifted***. If we wish to be more specific we add a phrase to the passive sentence and say *the rifle **was lifted** by the soldier*. The sentence makes sense without this phrase (*the rifle **was lifted***) but it doesn't convey as much information as the active form (*the soldier **lifted** his rifle*). If we add the phrase *by the soldier* we convey the same meaning as the active form but we use more words: seven (*the rifle **was lifted** by the soldier*) instead of five (*the soldier **lifted** his rifle*).

Other examples:

Capitalism enslaved the proletariat. (active)
The proletariat was enslaved. (passive)
Phar Lap won the Melbourne Cup. (active)
The Melbourne Cup was won. (passive)

(See also **Subject** and **Object**.)

Appendix 4

Solutions to activities

Chapter 7

3. *Punctuate the following sentences:*
   Shes here and its possible to ask her to help debug
   Johns program. Its problems arent too hard for her.

   She's here and it's possible to ask her to help debug John's
   program. Its problems aren't too hard for her.

4. *Change the following sentences from passive to active voice:*
   Passive: It was a warm day; her coat was put in the
   closet.

   Active: It was a warm day; she put her coat in the closet.

   Passive: Ayesha was given a high mark for her essay.

   Active: The tutor gave Ayesha a high mark for her essay.

   Passive: The table was surrounded by chairs.

   Active: Chairs surrounded the table.

Chapter 8

Hypothesis: Migrant men were more likely to be employed in
manufacturing industries in 1986 than the native-born men.

   Data from the 1986 Census
   • Number of men in employment: 3 951 903
   • Number of overseas-born men in employment: 1 036 918
   • Number of men working in manufacturing industries:
     714 351
   • Number of overseas-born men working in manufacturing
     industries: 250 226.

You only have data on men so you can't test the hypothesis
for all people, only for males. We need a table showing male
employment in manufacturing industry by birth place. (We can
work out the figures for Australian-born men by subtracting the
overseas-born from the totals.) Let's rough out the table and put in
the figures that we have got.

Table 1: Employment in manufacturing industries by birthplace, men, Australia 1986

Employment:	Australian-born	Overseas-born	Total
Employed in manufacturing	?	250 226	714 351
Employed in other industries	?	?	?
Total	?	1 036 918	3 951 903

Source: *Census 86 – Cross-Classified Characteristics* (1986: 121, 122)

When you are roughing out the table you do need to think. What is the independent variable and the dependent variable? How can I split each of them into at least two categories? When you've solved these problems the rest follows fairly automatically. Simple addition and subtraction allow you to fill in the empty cells.

Table 1: Employment in manufacturing industries by birthplace, men, Australia 1986

Employment:	Australian-born	Overseas-born	Total
Employed in manufacturing	464 125	250 226	714 351
Employed in other industries	2 450 860	786 692	3 237 552
Total	2 914 985	1 036 918	3 951 903

Source: Derived from *Census 86 – Cross-Classified Characteristics* (1986: 121, 122)

It's not yet possible to test the hypothesis that migrants were more likely to be employed in manufacturing industries than the Australian-born. The raw figures show that there were more Australian-born men in manufacturing industries in 1986 than there were migrant men, but there were also more Australian-born men in employment overall. So, you need to percentage Table 1. And of course, you will percentage it in the direction of the independent variable.

Table 2: Employment in manufacturing industries by birthplace, men, Australia 1986 (percentages)

Employment:	Australian-born	Overseas-born	Total
Employed in manufacturing	15.9	24.1	18.1
Employed in other industries	84.1	75.9	81.9
Total	100.0	100.0	100.0
Total N ('000s)	2 914 985	1 036 918	3 951 903

Source: Derived from Table 1

The result? The hypothesis is confirmed. Even though most men working in manufacturing were Australian-born, and even though most migrant men did not work in manufacturing, migrant men were more likely to work in manufacturing than Australian-born men.

You could not have tested the hypothesis by percentaging in the direction of the grand total, and working in the direction of the dependent variable would have brought bizarre results.

Appendix 5

English expression

Words that are often confused:

- its/it's
- affect/effect
- lie/lay
- uninterested/disinterested
- imply/infer
- they're/their/there
- principal/principle
- compliment/complement
- whose/who's
- fewer/less
- loose/lose
- accept/except

These words are arranged in a hierarchy. The ones that are most often confused in undergraduate essays come first.

The its/it's pair is discussed in Chapter 7 on pp.108–9. The following examples illustrate the correct use of each of the words in the list. If, after looking at these examples, you are still confused begin by looking up the words in a dictionary. If this is inadequate then move on to books like Murray-Smith (1987), Strumf and Douglas (2004), or Strunk, White and Angell (2000). Examples of correct usage follow:

The *effect* on the children of being separated from their parents *affected* the result of our observations of their behaviour at play. They showed a high level of *affect* (or feeling) when they were reunited with their parents. They cried with relief. But the *effect* of the emotion soon dissipated.

When I get home I will *lie* down and Stephen will *lay* the table.

Every day when I get home I *lie* down while Stephen *lays* the table.

I am *lying* down while Stephen is *laying* the table.

Yesterday I *lay* down when I got home and Stephen *laid* the table.

I have *lain* in bed all day; Stephen has *laid* the table.

(The verb *to lie* is intransitive; *to lay* is transitive. Confusion arises because the simple past tense of *to lie* is *lay*, as in: 'Yesterday I *lay* down.' See also *to fall* and *to fell* under *Intransitive* in Appendix 3.)

There is a scandal at the City Council. Some critics argue that the Mayor's decision to rezone the park for industrial development is not *disinterested*. They say he has shares in the development company. Despite the voters's anxiety, the local paper appears completely *uninterested*. Is the editor's lack of interest *disinterested*? Or does he have shares too?

The journalist did not mean to *imply* that the company was on the verge of bankruptcy but some readers *inferred* this from the article.

They're going to sell *their* surfboards when they get *there*.

The *principal* made a point of telling the children the first, or *principal*, reason for her pride in their work. She was using the *principle* that praise is more effective than criticism.

I like *compliments* when I cook. Pepper is essential in this recipe; it *complements* the flavour of the capsicums. It completes the dish.

'*Who's* going to help me plant the wheat?' said the little red hen. The chickens, *whose* thoughts were elsewhere, did not answer.

Let's make this cake with *fewer* almonds and *less* sugar than the last one.

The screw is *loose*. Watch out, or you'll *lose* it.

George *accepted* all the tasks *except* making the coffee. He felt that this duty should be *excepted* from the position description for his job.

The use of hopefully

'Hopefully' is often used, innocently and confidently, by writers who mean 'I hope' or 'if all goes well'. Alas! All may go very ill. These hopeful innocents can be engulfed by anger and vitriol flung at them by traditionalists who say that 'hopefully' has a different meaning. It means 'full of hope'. To avoid needless conflict do not use 'hopefully' where you mean 'I hope'. Keep it for the dear old sentence: 'It is better to travel hopefully than to arrive' (or, live dangerously and hopefully if you want to).

Stephen Murray-Smith tells us that we can play it safe if we avoid beginning a sentence with the word. The same advice applies to 'thankfully', 'mercifully' and others of their kind. (See Murray-Smith, 1987: 153.)

'Foreign' plurals

If you are using a word with a foreign origin, like 'forum' (taken from Latin) or 'octopus' (taken from Greek), don't try to give it a Latin or Greek plural. These words are now accepted as English and we have forums and octopuses. Besides, the 'correct' foreign plural of words borrowed from other languages can be tricky. If students guess that the Greek plural of 'octopus' might be 'octopi' they would be wrong. It's 'octopodes'. So, when writing English, stick to English.

There are a few exceptions to this rule. With the following words the plural from the foreign languages (Latin or Greek) is used:
* criterion/criteria
* datum/data
* medium/media
* phenomenon/phenomena
* stratum/strata

Often people only know the plural form (criteria, data, media, phenomena or strata) and they assume that the word is singular. They write 'The data is clear' or 'The data shows the following', instead of 'The data are clear' or 'The data show the following'. You may decide that this practice is so widespread that you should do the same. Why be a pedant? The language changes. But we want to make sure that you know what you are doing.

If an author writes that 'the media is under foreign control' or 'this phenomena is interesting', educated readers will always pick these uses as mistakes. Write this instead: 'The early years of the third millennium witnessed an unexpected phenomenon. Australian ownership of Australian press and telecommunications grew and the local media are now under local control.' (The grammar is acceptable but we don't claim that the sentence is accurate.)

References

A Guide to Australian Social Statistics (1993), Australian Bureau of Statistics, Canberra (Catalogue No. 4160.0).

Abercrombie, N., & Turner, B. (1978), 'The dominant ideology thesis', *British Journal of Sociology*, vol. 29, no. 2, pp. 149–170.

Abercrombie, N., Hill, S., & Turner, B. (2000), *The Penguin Dictionary of Sociology*, 4th edition, Penguin, London.

Australian Labour Market Statistics, April (2005), Australian Bureau of Statistics, Canberra, Catalogue No. 6105.0.

Bale, J., & Cronin, M. (2003), 'Introduction: sport and postcolonialism', in J. Bale and M. Cronin (Eds), *Sport and Postcolonialism*, Berg, Oxford.

Berger, P. (1966), *An Invitation to Sociology*, Penguin, Harmondsworth.

Betts, K., Hayward, D., & Garnham, N. (2001), *Quantitative Analysis in the Social Sciences: an Introduction*, Tertiary Press, Melbourne.

Boreham, P., Stokes, G., & Hall, R. (2004), *The Politics of Australian Society: Political Issues for the New Century*, Pearson Education Australia, Frenchs Forest, NSW.

Bouma, G. (2004), *The Research Process*, 5th Edition, Oxford University Press, Melbourne.

Bulbeck, C. (1993), *Social Sciences in Australia: An Introduction*, Harcourt Brace Jovanovich, Sydney.

Burke, G., & Spaull, A. (2002), 'Australian schools: participation and funding 1901–2001', *Year Book Australia, 2002*, Australian Bureau of Statistics, Canberra, Catalogue No. 1301.0 http://www.abs.gov.au/Ausstats/ accessed 19 May 2005.

Catalogue of Publications and Products (various years), Australian Bureau of Statistics, Canberra (Catalogue no. 1101.0).

Census 86 – Cross-Classified Characteristics of Persons and Dwellings: Australia (1986), Australian Bureau of Statistics, Canberra (Catalogue no. 2498.0).

Chamberlain, C. (1983), *Class Consciousness in Australia*, George Allen and Unwin, Sydney.

Connell, R. (1977), *Ruling Class, Ruling Culture*, Cambridge University Press, Cambridge.

de Vaus, D.A. (2002), *Surveys in Social Research*, 5th Edition, Allen and Unwin, Sydney.

Dykes, B. (1992), *Grammar Made Easy*, Hale and Iremonger, Sydney.

Ellis, J. (1989), *Against Deconstruction*, Princeton University Press, Princeton.

Esterberg, K. (2002), *Qualitative Methods in Social Research*, McGraw Hill, Boston.

Foddy, W. (1993), *Constructing Questions for Interview and Questionnaires: Theory and Practice in Social Research*, Cambridge University Press, Cambridge.

Foddy, W. (1988), *Elementary Applied Statistics for the Social Sciences*, Sydney, Harper and Row.

Giddens, A. (2001), *Sociology*, 4th Edition, Polity Press, Cambridge.

Goffman, E. (1971), *The Presentation of Self in Everyday Life*, Penguin, Harmondsworth.

Gonick, L., & Smith, W. (1993), *The Cartoon Guide to Statistics*, Harper Collins, New York.

Gouldner, A. (1979), *The Future of Intellectuals and the Rise of the New Class*, Seabury Press, New York.

Haralambos, M. (1985), *Sociology: Themes and Perspectives*, Bell and Hyman, London.

Hardin, R. (2001), 'Conceptions and explanations of trust', in K. Cook (Ed.), *Trust in Society*, Vol. II, Russell Sage Foundation, New York.

Hofstadter, D. (1982), '"Default assumptions" and their effects on writing and thinking', *Scientific American*, vol. 247, no. 5, pp. 14–21.

Holmes, D., Hughes, K., & Julian, R. (2003), *Australian Sociology: A Changing Society*, Pearson Longman, Frenchs Forest, NSW.

Judd, C., Smith, E., & Kidder, L. (1991), *Research Methods in Social Relations*, Holt, Rinehart and Winston, Fort Worth.

Kellehear, A. (1993), *The Unobtrusive Researcher: A Guide to Methods*, Allen and Unwin, Sydney.

Macionis, J. (2004), *Society: The Basics*, Prentice Hall, Upper Saddle, NJ.

Macionis, J., & Plummer, K. (2002), *Sociology: A Global Introduction*, Prentice Hall, New York.

Maher, C., & Burke, T. (1991), *Informed Decision-Making: The Use of Secondary Data Sources in Policy Studies*, Longman Cheshire, Melbourne.

Mann, M. (1972), 'The social cohesion of liberal democracy', in M. Mankoff (Ed.), *The Poverty of Progress: The Political Economy of American Social Problems*, Holt, Rinehart and Winston, New York.

Mannheim, K. (1936), *Ideology and Utopia: An Introduction to the Sociology of Knowledge*, Routledge and Kegan Paul, London.

McLean, I., & MacMillan, A. (2003), *The Concise Oxford Dictionary of Politics*, Oxford University Press, Oxford.

Melbourne: Facts and Figures (n.d.), Victorian Government Publishing Office with the Ministry for Planning and Environment, and the Australian Bureau of Statistics, Melbourne.

Mills, C.W. (1970), *The Sociological Imagination*, Penguin, Harmondsworth.

Mills, J., & Dimeo, P. (2003), '"When gold fires it shines": sport, imagination and the body in colonial and postcolonial India', in J. Bale and M. Cronin (Eds), *Sport and Postcolonialism*, Berg, Oxford.

Murray-Smith, S. (1987), *Right Words*, Viking, Ringwood.

National Statistical Systems: A Guided Tour (1992), Australian Bureau of Statistics, Canberra (Catalogue no. 1130.0).

Neuman, W.L. (2003), *Social Research Methods: Qualitative and Quantitative Approaches*, Pearson Education, Boston.

Popper, K.R. (1976), 'Reason or revolution?' in T.W. Adorno, H. Albert, R. Dahrendorf, J. Habermas, H. Pilot and K.R. Popper, *The Positivist Dispute in German Sociology* (translated by G. Adey and D. Frisby), Heinemann, London.

Richards, L. (1978), *Having Families: Marriage, Parenthood and Social Pressure in Australia*, Penguin, Ringwood.

Robertson, I. (1989), *Society: A Brief Introduction*, Worth, New York.

Schools 2004 (2005), Australian Bureau of Statistics, Canberra, Catalogue no. 4221.0.

Shorter, E. (1975), *The Making of the Modern Family*, Basic Books, New York.

Snooks & Co. (2002), *Style Manual for Authors, Editors and Printers*, John Wiley and Sons, Brisbane.

Social Indicators (1992), Australian Bureau of Statistics, Canberra (Catalogue number 4101.0).

Social Sciences Index (The H.W. Wilson Company, New York).

Sociological Abstracts (Sociological Abstracts Inc., San Diego).

Statistics – a Powerful Edge! (1998), Australian Bureau of Statistics, Canberra, Catalogue no. 1331.0.

Strumf, M., & Douglas, A. (2004), *The Grammar Bible: Everything You Always Wanted to Know About Grammar but Didn't Know Whom to Ask*, Owl Books, New York.

Strunk, W., White, E.B., & Angell, R. (2000), *The Elements of Style*, Longman, New York.

Sudman, S., & Bradburn, N. (1982), *Asking Questions*, Jossey-Bass, San Francisco.

The Nuttall Dictionary of English Synonyms and Antonyms (1943), Frederick Warne, London.

Thompson, J.B. (1984), *Studies in the Theory of Ideology*, Cambridge, Polity Press.

Truss, L. (2003), *Eats, Shoots & Leaves: The Zero Tolerance Approach to Punctuation*, London, Profile Books.

Viviani, N. (1984), *The Long Journey: Vietnamese Migrations and Settlement in Australia*, Melbourne University Press, Melbourne.

Wadsworth, Y. (1997), *Do It Yourself Social Research, 2nd Edition*, Allen and Unwin, Sydney.

Willis, E. (2004), *The Sociological Quest: An Introduction to the Study of Social Life*, Allen and Unwin, Sydney.

Index